The Liturgical Home

CHRISTMAS

Ashley Tumlin Wallace

ANGLICAN
COMPASS

CONTENTS

Foreword   vii
Preface   ix

1. HOW TO USE THIS BOOK   1
What are the Church seasons?   1
What is Christmas?   1
How to Celebrate Christmas   2
Christmas Traditions for the Entire Season   2
Christmas Traditions for Specific Days   2
Christmas Devotions   3
Christmas Recipes   3

2. WHAT ARE THE SEASONS OF THE
CHURCH?   5

3. WHAT IS THE SEASON OF CHRISTMAS?   9

4. HOW TO CELEBRATE CHRISTMAS   13
Ideas for Personal or Family Commitments
During Christmastide   14
Putting It All Together   16

5. CHRISTMAS TRADITIONS FOR THE
ENTIRE SEASON   17
Advent Wreath   18
Christmas Baking   20
Christmas Carols and Music   21
Christmas Caroling   22
Christmas Colors   23
Christmas Crib   24
Christmas Flowers and Plants   25
Christmas Foods   27
Christmas Gifts   28
Christmas Greetings   30
Christmas Names   30

Christmas Ornaments 31
Christmas Tree 32
Christmas Wreath 33
Manger 33
Nativity Scene or Crèche 34
Light 35
Stockings 36
The Paradise Tree 37
The Star of Bethlehem 38
Yule Log 38

6. CHRISTMAS TRADITIONS FOR SPECIFIC
   DAYS 41
Christmas Eve (December 24) 42
The Feast of the Nativity, Christmas Day
(December 25) 56
The Feast of Saint Stephen (December 26) 59
The Feast of Saint John (December 27) 62
The Feast of the Holy Innocents (December
28) 65
New Year's Eve or Saint Sylvester's Day
(December 31st) 67
The Feast of the Holy Name or New Year's
Day (January 1st) 68
Twelfth Night (January 5th) 70
The Feast of the Epiphany (January 6th) 75
The Season of Epiphany or Epiphanytide 77

7. CHRISTMAS DEVOTIONS 79
December 24, Christmas Eve 79
December 25, Christmas Day 84
December 26, The Feast of St. Stephen 87
December 27, The Feast of St. John 91
December 28, The Feast of the Holy
Innocents 94
December 29 97
December 30 100
December 31 (New Year's Eve) 103
January 1, The Feast of the Holy Name 106

January 2   109
January 3   111
January 4   114
January 5   117

8. CHRISTMASTIDE RECIPES   121
Bubble and Squeak   121
Buche de Noel or Christmas Log   123
Bunuelos (Mexican Fritters)   125
Chickadee Pudding   128
Christmas Punch   129
Christmas Punch for Children   130
Coventry God Cakes   130
Eggnog   132
Fruitcake   134
Knodel (Potato Dumplings)   135
Kourabiedes (Greek Butter Cookies)   137
Krapfen   139
Lamb's Wool   142
Mexican Hot Chocolate   143
Mulled Ale   144
Mulled Cider   145
Panettone (Italian Christmas Bread)   146
Passatelli in Brodo   148
Pernil   150
Ponche (Mexican Christmas Punch)   152
Rice Cakes with Louisiana Syrup (Cane Syrup)   153
Roast Goose   154
St. John's Wine   156
St. Stephen's Horseshoes   156
Stollen   159
Sylvester Punch   162
Tamales   163
Three Kings Cake or Rosca de Reyes   165
Wassail   168

FOREWORD

～

AT ANGLICAN COMPASS, we help you navigate with clarity and charity, pointing to Christ as the way, the truth, and the life.

The Church calendar is a way of life—a rhythm that's meant to form our families and our friendships. But how do we live it out on the ground, in our homes? What does The Liturgical Home look like? To answer that question, it really helps to have a good friend who can speak from experience. And Ashley is a great friend, with abundant experience from many years making a home with her husband and their four children.

In the pages that follow, let Ashley be your guide, a source of new ideas (and recipes!) for observing The Liturgical

Home with family and friends. You will have a lot of fun along the way. And even more important, you will grow closer to Jesus.

PREFACE

~

"For everything there is a season" *Ecclesiastes 3:1.*

Growing up in the South, I didn't know a lot about seasons. I mean, I knew about them from books and movies, but I had never really experienced them. The only seasons we had in the Florida panhandle were kind of hot, hot, and very hot.

When my husband was given the opportunity to attend seminary in Wisconsin, we were nervous to leave our home and family but we were also excited to be making such a radical change and to experience a world filled with seasons that were completely alien to us.

The fall in Wisconsin was beyond anything we could have imagined. Brilliant reds, golds, oranges, and yellows exploded from the trees. Every scene took your breath away, every view looked like a postcard picture. Hooray for seasons! Hooray for us being wild and adventurous! Little did we know, falls in Wisconsin are short-lived and winter comes all too quickly!

In the winter of 2002, I found myself far from the life I once knew. Here I was, a beach girl transplanted to the frosty climes of Wisconsin. For those of you who have never experienced a Wisconsin winter, let me explain: you don't leave the house . . . ever! It is just too cold! Especially when you're from Florida! And seeing as how I had just given birth to my second child, we were housebound in a major way. I felt very isolated and I was left with a lot of time to think. I thought deep thoughts like, "Who am I?" "What is my purpose in the world?" and the much more desperate, **"WHAT IN THE WORLD AM I DOING IN WISCONSIN?"**

The days were so long and cold. It felt like I did the same thing every day. There seemed to be very little structure to my life and my days felt monotonous and without form. We were Christians so we read Bible stories to our children, we talked to them about Jesus and we sang Christian songs with them but that filled up a very small portion of the day. It just didn't seem like enough to me. I wanted a lot more meaning in my day. I had a deep desire to incorporate the things of God more into my life. I wanted my everyday life to be permeated with the Spirit of the living God.

One night as I was reading a local magazine, I was drawn to an interview with a new chef from a restaurant in nearby Milwaukee. He was describing the foods that he was currently serving. They were all traditional Advent foods from his small village in France. I was so intrigued. I had no idea that other countries and other cultures had particular foods that they made for Advent and Christmas.

A chef who was preparing traditional Advent foods from his village in France? I wondered how many more traditions other cultures have. How many other ways have people celebrated the seasons of the church? I wanted to find out more.

This was an entirely new concept to me that a whole region could be so shaped by the traditions of their faith. I loved it. I started asking a lot of questions and doing a lot of research.

This whole world opened up to me—a world of possibilities. People around the world were living out their faith with traditions that were similar but with regional and ethnic differences based on foods and geographic regions. It reminded me of St. Paul's analogy about the body of Christ in 1 Corinthians. We are all uniquely made and yet we are all one body of Christ.

I began to think about my own little family. Who are we as a family within the larger framework of Christians? What traditions do I want to embrace? I began to get so excited. What if my day could ebb and flow with the greater life of the church? What if my day could be filled with meaning, richness, color, taste . . . things that involve all of our senses? What if I could create an atmosphere of faith in my home, traditions that enriched and gave structure, purpose, and unity with the local church and then the wider, worldwide church? Themes of wholeness and identity began to take shape in my heart.

I started researching and collecting traditions from all over the world. I compiled them all, and I incorporated these traditions into my own family. During the season of Christmas, we celebrate the birth of Jesus not just on Christmas Day but for twelve whole days! Twelve days of feasting and singing with abandon all of the beautiful Christmas carols we didn't sing during Advent. We bake cookies, make rich desserts, and light the Christ candle in the middle of our Advent wreath! This is what celebrating Christmas for twelve days does; it takes the chaos and the frantic rush of our lives and forces us to slow down. As a family, we are given time to fully celebrate the birth of Christ for twelve whole days!

What you hold in your hand is the result of my journey through the seasons of the Church. I hope it will bless you as a resource and as a guide through your own journey. Here's to embracing all that the seasons of the Church have to offer!

Truly,

Ashley Wallace

HOW TO USE THIS BOOK

*I*n the Liturgical Home, you will encounter beautiful traditions and celebrations from all over the world. I hope they will bless you on your journey through the seasons of the Church Year.

WHAT ARE THE CHURCH SEASONS?

For those new to liturgical living, we have included a brief introduction to the Church seasons.

WHAT IS CHRISTMAS?

In this chapter, you will be introduced to the season of Christmastide and the traditional ways it has been celebrated worldwide.

HOW TO CELEBRATE CHRISTMAS

Because our culture celebrates Christmas differently from the Church, we've included suggestions about preparing ourselves for Christmas as individuals and as families.

CHRISTMAS TRADITIONS FOR THE ENTIRE SEASON

Some Christmas traditions, such as singing Christmas Carols and feasting, last for the entire season. This section contains ideas for celebrating Christmas throughout the season.

CHRISTMAS TRADITIONS FOR SPECIFIC DAYS

Other Christmas traditions, such as celebrating the Feast of St. John (December 27th) or the Feast of the Holy Innocents (December 28), only apply to specific days. Check this section for Christmastide traditions for particular days.

Remember that none of these Christmas ideas are mandates. Be realistic in your selections. Choose observances that seem interesting and manageable. It is not necessary to do all of them. The ideas are not meant to be a burden or to cause stress. They are meant to be a blessing to you and a way to unify you with your friends, your family, your church, and the church universal as we move through the seasons of the Church.

CHRISTMAS DEVOTIONS

We have included devotions for each day of Christmas. We hope that these devotions will help guide you in prayer. They have been designed to be easy to use and understand. Decide on the right time to have a devotion. Right before or after dinner or before bed is often the best time.

If more than one person participates in the devotions, invite different members to be the leader, read the readings, or light the candles. In families, it can be fun to allow the children to lead the devotions occasionally.

CHRISTMAS RECIPES

Sugar cookies are just the beginning! Christmas is twelve full days of feasting! This section will teach you how to make everything from St. Stephen's Horseshoes to Mulled Wine.

WHAT ARE THE SEASONS OF THE CHURCH?

*T*he faith of God's people throughout the history of Israel and the Church has been holistic. It was a faith that encompassed all areas of the people's lives and ebbed and flowed with the changing seasons. Their faith was individual; however, just as important, it was corporate. Everyone celebrated the same festivals and rituals together, giving them a sense of belonging to something bigger than themselves. Theirs was also an experiential faith that involved all of their senses with the use of incense, eating and abstaining from certain foods, hearing and teaching of the Word of God, and singing spiritual songs.

In this way, for the Jewish people, time became much more than just what the Greeks called *chronos—the passing of time as a measurable quantity of days, weeks,* and years. Celebrating the festivals and rituals of their faith sanctified the *chronos* of their lives and made it *kairos*. This time is not measured by its duration but rather by its quality and significance. The festivals and rituals reminded them daily that God had chosen them to be his people and that their relationship with him and nothing else gave their lives significance.

When the long-awaited Messiah finally came in the person of Jesus, everything changed for those who believed in him. The old festivals told only the first part of the story. Now, a new kairos had dawned, and new celebrations were necessary. The creation of the Seasons of the Church, the liturgical calendar that begins each year with the First Sunday of Advent, was the natural and beautiful response to the coming of the Messiah. He was the fulfillment of Holy Scripture and the consummation of all hopes and desires. The Church experienced Christ's resurrection as the ultimate fulfillment of all things God promised, so new celebrations were created.

The earliest record of what would later develop into the seasons of the Church calendar is the Early Church's celebration of Christ's death and resurrection. Saint Irenaeus, who lived during the second century A.D., claimed that the celebration of Christ's death and resurrection went back to the time of Saint Polycarp, a disciple of the Apostle John. This means that the Church had already begun to celebrate the life of Jesus from the very earliest of times.

Consequently, an entire liturgical year was created to walk the Church, both corporately and individually, through Jesus' life and ministry. The Church's faith was not something upheld and taught only on Sundays; it was something each member of the Church lived every day. It was an experience.

Through the reading of Scripture, the celebration of the Eucharist, and the observance of the feast days and fast days, we celebrate the most significant events in the life of Christ and the life of the Church. We are constantly molded and shaped as we walk through these seasons. The Church's seasons don't just repeat; they reshape and reform us, making us more and more like Jesus. In other words, the seasons of the Church are how we are shaped into God's people.

As we move through the seasons of the Church, we continuously marvel at what God has done for us through his holy son, Jesus Christ. He has made a way back to him, back to abundant life. Because we are so filled with gratitude, we want to serve and honor God not just on Sundays but every day with every part of our lives. The seasons of the Church were created so that our everyday lives would be permeated with the Spirit of the Living God. The seasons do not take precedence over interior formation but are a means of enrichment.

This book was written to help you move into a deeper, daily walk with God. By incorporating the seasons of the Church into our lives, we can honor God more intentionally with our lives, and we can move not only individually but also as a family, as a church, and as the Church Universal through the life and mysteries of Christ.

May you be richly blessed as you embrace this marvelous gift—the seasons of the Church.

WHAT IS THE SEASON OF CHRISTMAS?

*T*he anticipation, preparation, and longing of Advent culminate in the Nativity, where the promise of God to send a Savior is fulfilled. The prophets foretold of a Messiah who would bring salvation, and their voices echo through the ages, leading us to the humble stable in Bethlehem. There, in the quiet of the night, the King of Kings is born not in a grand palace but in a manger, surrounded by the simplicity of shepherds and the songs of angels. This is the profound mystery of the Incarnation—God with us, Emmanuel.

Christmas is the time set aside to celebrate and reflect on the miracle of Jesus' birth and its significance in our lives. It is a period of rejoicing in the Light that has come into the world to dispel darkness. The celebration is not confined to a single day but spans twelve days, each offering an opportunity to meditate on the gifts and graces that Christ brings. These days are filled with joy, feasting, and celebrating, echoing the angelic proclamation of "good news of great joy for all people."

The symbolism of the Twelve Days of Christmas is rich with meaning. Each day represents a different aspect of the Christian faith, from the calling of the apostles to the gifts of the Holy Spirit. This period is a time to immerse ourselves in the depths of God's love and to contemplate the great gift of Jesus, who comes to reconcile us to the Father. As the world moves quickly past Christmas, returning to the routines of daily life, the Church remains in a state of celebration, cherishing the extended time to honor Christ's birth.

During Christmas, we are reminded of the humble beginnings of our Savior and the profound impact of his arrival. It also invites us to consider the reality of Christ's presence in our lives today. The Incarnation is not just a historical event but a living reality. Jesus is continually being born anew in our hearts, calling us to live in the light of his love and grace. Christmastide is a time to deepen our relationship with him, to allow his presence to transform our lives, and to share his love with others.

As we celebrate the Twelve Days of Christmas, let us also remember those who are less fortunate. Just as there was no room at the inn for the Holy Family, many today find themselves without shelter, warmth, or comfort. This season calls us to act compassionately, extending our hands and hearts to those in need. By doing so, we honor the true spirit of Christmas and embody the love of Christ in tangible ways.

As God's people, let us reclaim the beauty and wonder of Christmas, celebrating it with the Church worldwide. Hear these words from the Christmas liturgy, which capture the essence of this holy season:

Almighty God, you have given your only-begotten Son to take our nature upon him, and to be born [this day] of a pure virgin: Grant that we, who have been born again and made your children by adoption and grace, may daily be renewed by your Holy Spirit; through our Lord Jesus Christ, to whom with you and the same Spirit be honor and glory, now and for ever. *Amen*

As we journey through these twelve days, may our hearts be filled with the joy and peace of Christ. Let us sing with the angels, rejoice with the shepherds, and seek with the Magi, always remembering that the greatest gift we receive and give is the love of God made manifest in Jesus. May Christmas be a time of deep spiritual renewal and an outpouring of love as we celebrate the wondrous mystery of the Incarnation and the everlasting hope it brings to the world.

HOW TO CELEBRATE CHRISTMAS

*P*roperly observed, the traditional Christian observance of the Christmas season radically differs from how most of us celebrate Christmas. Most of us celebrate Christmas Day, remove all signs of Christmas from our homes, and then move on with our everyday lives.

But the Church believes that the birth of Jesus is so miraculous and pivotal to our faith that a whole season of feasting is devoted to it. Christmas begins on Christmas Eve and is a period of celebration and feasting that lasts for twelve whole days! We leave up all of our Christmas decorations, and for twelve days, we celebrate and enjoy all that God has done for us through Jesus.

IDEAS FOR PERSONAL OR FAMILY COMMITMENTS DURING CHRISTMASTIDE

Personal or family commitments help us set this time apart as holy and to prepare our hearts.

Prepare Together.

Commit to preparing your home for Christmas. Incorporate the five senses into your home. Put out a candle that reminds you of Christmas. Create a Christmas playlist with all of your favorite Christmas carols. Cook some of the Christmastide recipes found at the back of the book. Add seasonal decor to your home that reminds you of Christmas.

Use liturgical color in your home. In the fourth century, the Western church began using colors to differentiate liturgical seasons. The colors were created to give a visual cue to everyone in attendance as to what season they were celebrating. The liturgical colors for the season of Christmastide are white and gold. White symbolizes purity and holiness, and gold symbolizes royalty. The liturgical color also changes for special days throughout the season and will be noted in the book.

Eat Together.

Decide how many times you will eat together during the week, and try to stick to this commitment. Make sure that no devices are allowed at the table. When you eat together, pick something that everyone will enjoy so there is no strife at the table. Take your time eating the meal and explain to your children that even though they might be done eating, they will remain at the table to share in the family time.

Feast Together.

Christmastide is all about feasting, so feast together as a family! What would it look like for your family to feast for twelve days?

Pray Together.

Find a time for devotions that best suits your family: at the breakfast table, around the table after dinner, in the children's bedroom right before bed, etc. Give your children roles to play in your time of devotion. Allow them to light the candles, snuff out the candles, read the scriptures, pray, pick the song you sing, etc. This is a beautiful way to show your children that they are an important part of God's family and to help them feel included.

Serve Together.

Since Christmastide is all about joyful celebrations and feasting, think about ways your family could share the joy of Jesus' birth with those around you. As a family, visit those you know who are shut-ins, widowers, or widows. Care for the orphans and the poor among you. Invite people over for a festive meal. Do something kind for the staff at your church, particularly the clergy. They are exhausted after the Christmas Eve and Christmas Day services and could use some joy and appreciation!

PUTTING IT ALL TOGETHER

Decide personally or as a family how you will mark this time. Make it official by writing down your commitments and hanging them prominently in your home, like on the refrigerator or the kitchen wall.

If you have children, allow them to decorate your commitments with things that remind them of Christmas, such as the Christmas colors, a Christmas wreath, the Holy Family, or the particular family commitments you have made.

Talk to your children about how the family will walk through Christmastide. Explain to them that how you walk through this time as a family will look very different from how the world behaves during this time of the year. Remind them that everything you do during Christmastide is done to celebrate the birth of Jesus. We celebrate the birth of Jesus not only in our hearts but also in our lives.

Remind them that celebrating Christmastide is something we do for ourselves to help us sanctify the time and remember who we are and what Jesus has done for us. It does not help God love us more, nor will it make him love us any less. He already loves each of us more than we can imagine.

CHRISTMAS TRADITIONS FOR THE ENTIRE SEASON

*N*umerous time-honored traditions help us observe Christmas, each serving as a meaningful way to focus our hearts and minds on this sacred season. Many people think that Christmas traditions end on Christmas Day, but this is not the case. So leave your Advent Wreath out, and don't take down your Christmas tree! We keep these beautiful traditions going for twelve glorious days!

These practices are meant to enrich your family's celebration, marking the days with intentionality and joy. Choose the ones that resonate with you, but remember not to take on too much—these traditions are here to deepen your experience, not to overwhelm you. Once you've selected a few, weave them into your daily and weekly devotions, allowing them to enhance your journey through the Christmas season.

ADVENT WREATH

Don't put away your Advent Wreath yet! During the 12 Days of Christmas, we continue lighting all the candles in the wreath, including the white Christ candle in the middle!

And if you are unfamiliar with the tradition of the Advent Wreath:

The Advent Wreath is a wreath of evergreens with equidistant candles and a central candle. The wreath is a wonderful visual symbol marking our passage of time through Advent. The Advent Wreath provides a visual focus for your evening family devotions.

The wreath is used as a sign to your family that Christians are joyfully waiting for the coming of our Savior, the Christ Child, as every Sunday in Advent, a new candle is lit. Make an Advent Wreath from a kit or on your own, hang it from the ceiling, or place it in the center of your dining table. Gather your family every Sunday night for Evening Prayer, light the appropriate number of candles, and pray through your family devotions.

The Advent wreath is full of beautiful symbols. The shape of the circle represents eternity. Evergreens are a traditional Christmas decoration that represents the eternal nature of God. Candles represent a time of preparation and purification as well as the light or presence of Christ. The color of the candles is also symbolic. Violet represents penitence as we prepare our hearts for the birth of our Savior. Blue is also used instead of violet to symbolize a sense of expectancy. The rose or pink candle represents Mary—God's willing servant and mother of our Lord. The white candle represents Christ and is lit on Christmas Eve.

The order in which each candle is lit is also symbolic.

The first candle is the Patriarch's Candle, which reminds us of the great patriarchs of the Bible who faithfully followed God and prepared for the coming of the Messiah. On this day, a violet or blue candle is lit.

The second candle is the Prophet's Candle, which reminds us of the great prophets of the Bible who faithfully followed God and called God's people to return to God and faithfulness. A violet or blue candle and the Patriarch's candle are lit on this day.

The third candle is the Virgin Mary Candle, which reminds us of Mary's faithfulness in responding to God's call to bear Christ. A rose or pink candle is lit along with the Patriarch's and the Prophet's candles.

Note: The third Sunday of Advent is often called Gaudete Sunday. Gaudete means rejoice! The opening antiphon for this day is "Rejoice in the Lord always," which in Latin is Gaudete in Domino Semper. On this day, the penitent mood lifts, and we move into a more joyful time of expectancy as the celebration of Christ's birth draws closer.

The fourth candle is the John the Baptist Candle. Jesus calls John the greatest of all prophets. He came to proclaim the coming of the Messiah and to prepare the way of the Lord. On this day, a violet or blue candle is lit along with the Patriarch's candle, the Prophet's Candle, and the Virgin Mary's Candle.

The fifth and central candle is the Christ Candle, which represents the birth of our Savior. It is lit on Christmas Eve. We continue to light it with the other four candles on Christmas Day and the subsequent twelve Days of Christmas.

CHRISTMAS BAKING

Christmastide is a wonderful time to bake with children. Baking helps to emphasize the themes of Christmas further: feasting, celebrating, and sharing our delicious treats with others. Around the world, there are incredible traditional cookies, breads, and desserts specifically made during the 12 Days of Christmas.

CHRISTMAS CAROLS AND MUSIC

During Advent, we sang Advent hymns filled with expectation and longing for the promised Savior. Now he is here, and it's time to celebrate by singing Christmas carols with abandon for 12 days!

Christmas music is filled with joy, celebration, and wonder, reflecting the beauty and mystery of Christ's birth. Unlike the reflective and expectant nature of Advent music, Christmas carols are marked by their jubilant melodies and lyrics that proclaim the arrival of the Savior. Songs like "Joy to the World" and "Hark! The Herald Angels Sing" burst forth with praise, celebrating Christ's entrance into the world and His role as the long-awaited King. The familiar sounds of bells, trumpets, and soaring choruses are hallmarks of the season, as they capture the overwhelming joy of God's gift to humanity.

One of the most iconic Christmas hymns is "Hark! The Herald Angels Sing," a classic English Christmas carol. The song is filled with rich theological themes, proclaiming the glory of Christ's birth and the reconciliation between God and humanity. The carol's celebratory tone and majestic melody make it a favorite for Christmas Eve and Christmas morning services, where it often accompanies the lighting of the Christ candle.

Another timeless Christmas carol is "Silent Night." First sung in Austria in 1818, this gentle and serene carol emphasizes the peace and stillness of the holy night when Christ was born. The melody and lyrics about the infant Savior sleeping peacefully bring a sense of quiet reverence to the season.

Handel's *Messiah* is one of the world's most renowned and celebrated pieces of music, especially associated with the Christmas season. Composed by George Frideric Handel in 1741, this oratorio has become a cornerstone of classical music and a beloved part of holiday traditions. Although initially intended for Easter, Messiah has become most closely linked with Christmas, particularly its "Hallelujah" chorus, one of the most recognizable and uplifting pieces of choral music ever written.

The 12 Days of Christmas is a traditional English Christmas carol that dates back to at least the 18th century. The song is structured as a cumulative list, with each verse building on the previous ones, recounting a series of increasingly grand gifts given on each of the twelve days of Christmas, which span from December 25th to January 5th, the eve of Epiphany. The gifts famously include items such as "five golden rings," "three French hens," and "a partridge in a pear tree," each symbolizing our walk through the Christmas season with abundance, generosity, and joy.

CHRISTMAS CAROLING

Christmas caroling is a beloved tradition that dates back to the Middle Ages. It brings communities together through the joyous singing of hymns and carols celebrating the birth of Christ.

Christmas caroling often involves a group of people visiting homes in their neighborhood, celebrating and sharing the good news of Christ's birth through songs. With their soaring melodies and rich theology, these songs spread the spirit of Christmas to everyone who hears them. In some communities, carolers are invited inside to warm up with hot cocoa or cider, making it a time of fellowship, connection, and musical celebration.

Caroling is more than just a festive activity; it's a way to proclaim the message of Christmas in a personal and communal way. Singing together in public spaces or at neighbors' doorsteps embodies the joy and generosity of the season.

CHRISTMAS COLORS

The traditional colors of Christmas—red, green, gold, and white—are rich in symbolism and have been used in Christian celebrations for centuries. Each color holds a deep meaning that reflects the joy and significance of the season.

Red represents the blood of Christ, shed for humanity's salvation. It reminds us of God's ultimate sacrifice and the love that Christ embodies. Red is often used in decorations, such as holly berries and poinsettias.

Green symbolizes eternal life, as it is the color of evergreens, which remain vibrant even in the depths of winter. Evergreen trees, wreaths, and garlands are commonly used to decorate homes and churches, representing the everlasting life that Christ offers.

Gold signifies God's glory, the world's light, and the season's splendor. It reminds us of the gifts of the Magi, particularly the gift of gold, which was given to honor the King of Kings. Gold is often used in ornaments, candle holders, and other decorations, adding a sense of warmth and majesty to Christmas celebrations.

White symbolizes purity, holiness, and the light of Christ. It is the color often associated with the angels and the innocence of the Christ child. White is prominently featured in Christmas liturgies and used in church decorations, such as altar cloths and vestments, during Christmas. It serves as a reminder of the purity of Christ and the call to holiness in our own lives.

CHRISTMAS CRIB

The manger that held baby Jesus is highly symbolic for Christians. It has a Eucharistic message: the manger that once held grain for the animals now holds the very Bread of Life. It is a powerful anticipation of the mystery of Holy Communion. In many countries, a large wooden crib or manger is placed in the living room on the first Sunday of Advent. The crib is empty, and a bag of straw is placed next to it. Every evening, after family prayers, the children in the family come to the crib and place one piece of straw in the crib for every sacrifice or good deed done that day. All these good deeds and sacrifices are done to please the Christ Child. The idea is to do as many good deeds as possible so that baby Jesus has a soft bed to lie on.

On Christmas Eve, the Christ Child figurine is lovingly added to the pile of straw created from the selfless acts of love towards others and remains out to be enjoyed for the 12 Days of Christmas.

In Poland, they have their own unique crib-making tradition. Their cribs don't resemble the modest managers you usually see; they look more like a castle or a church with towers shooting into the sky. Inside, you'll find the sleeping baby Jesus with figures of festively dressed townsfolk keeping watch from above. The Polish tradition of making these cribs is so remarkable that it has been added to the UNESCO list of intangible cultural heritage.

CHRISTMAS FLOWERS AND PLANTS

Christmas flowers are not only beautiful but also carry deep symbolic meanings that reflect the Christmas season. Some of the most beloved flowers used during Christmas are poinsettias, holly, and Christmas roses, each contributing to the festive atmosphere while reminding us of important aspects of the Christian faith.

Poinsettias are perhaps the most iconic Christmas flower. They are originally from Mexico, where they are known as "La Flor de Nochebuena" (Flower of the Holy Night). The poinsettia's star-shaped leaf pattern symbolizes the Star of Bethlehem, which led the wise men to Jesus. The vibrant red leaves represent the blood of Christ, while the white varieties symbolize purity and the hope of the Christmas season.

Poinsettias are associated with the legend of a poor girl who lived in Mexico. When Christmastime came, she longed to give baby Jesus a present, but she had no money. She broke off some branches from a bush growing by the side of the road, tied them in a bouquet, and laid them beside the crib in the church. The congregation was so surprised when the sprigs changed from green to red. It was a miracle.

Pohutukawa. Large red flowering bush that appears during Christmas along the coast of New Zealand. It is the flower for the season and appears everywhere. It even has a carol, "Aotearoa Christmas," which tells of Christmases spent on the beach in the shade of the pohutukawa tree.

Holly is another traditional Christmas plant with deep Christian symbolism. The sharp, pointed leaves represent the crown of thorns Christ wore during his crucifixion, while the red berries symbolize his blood. Holly is often used in wreaths and other decorations to foreshadow the Passion of Christ, even during the joyous celebration of his birth.

Christmas Roses, also known as the "Hellebore," are associated with a legend that tells of a young girl who had nothing to give the Christ child. According to the story, she was crying, and a beautiful white flower bloomed where her tears fell—the Christmas rose. This flower symbolizes purity and the hope that springs forth even in the darkest of times.

Rosemary, with its blue flowers, has always been associated with Christmas. Tradition has it that it was the bush used by Mary to dry baby Jesus' clothes. When she laid his clothes on the bush to dry, the white flowers of the bush miraculously changed to blue.

CHRISTMAS FOODS

Christmas is a season rich with culinary traditions that delight the senses and carry deep symbolic meanings tied to our faith. Each dish, enjoyed for centuries, tells a story connecting us to the celebration of Christ's birth.

Since the Middle Ages, the Christmas Goose has been a classic centerpiece of European Christmas feasts. Chosen for its availability as one of the last animals slaughtered before winter, the goose symbolizes abundance and is traditionally served at festive gatherings.

Fruitcake is another enduring treat. It is packed with dried fruits and nuts and often soaked in brandy or rum. Originally an indulgence due to the expense of its ingredients, fruitcake became a popular holiday gift, especially after becoming widely available by mail in the early 20th century.

Candy canes are a beloved Christmas treat, easily recognizable with their red and white stripes. Shaped like a shepherd's crook, they represent Jesus as the Good Shepherd. The red symbolizes His sacrifice, while the white stands for His purity, making candy canes a sweet reminder of Christ's love.

Stollen, a traditional German bread made since the Middle Ages, is often enjoyed during Christmas. The folded bread, with seams on top, is said to symbolize Christ's swaddling clothes, making it a meaningful addition to holiday celebrations.

CHRISTMAS GIFTS

In many countries, Christmas gifts are given on Christmas Eve or Christmas Day. However, there is also a strong tradition of giving a gift every day during the Twelve Days of Christmas. It is also important to note that in many Eastern countries, gift giving is reserved for Epiphany to celebrate the bringing of gifts by the Magi to the Christ Child.

A significant difference between the way the majority of the Christian world and the United States give gifts has to do with who is believed to give the gifts. In the United States, the historical figure of Saint Nicholas, whose feast day is celebrated on December 6, has largely been replaced by the fictitious character known as Santa Claus. Children are told that Santa Claus is responsible for all (or most) of the gifts on Christmas Day. However, in the rest of the Christian world, children are taught that the Christ Child decorates their Christmas tree and gives them all of their gifts.

Attributing all gifts to the Christ Child is a wonderful way to demonstrate to your children that "every good and perfect gift" comes from God and that the greatest of these gifts is Jesus, sent to save us from our sins and bring us back to God.

Make sure that you teach your children as they grow up that the focus of gift-giving should be on what we give rather than on what we receive. We give because God first freely gave to us. He held nothing back! He even gave us his most precious gift - his only Son. A great way to emphasize giving could be to encourage your children to make their gifts by hand. If every gift given by your children had been lovingly and thoughtfully handmade, how much more meaningful would they be?

Traditionally, Christmas gifts were given to the poor. Because Jesus humbled himself and became poor, the poor were the ones who were honored with gifts. Since Jesus said that everything we do for the poor, we do for him, have your family focus on collecting alms and buying them gifts.

CHRISTMAS GREETINGS

Christmas is celebrated with joy around the world. As soon as the season begins on Christmas Eve, each culture has its own unique way of expressing the festive spirit through traditional greetings.

In English, it is "Merry Christmas."

In Spanish-speaking countries, it is "Feliz Navidad."

In Italian it is "Buon Natale."

In France it is "Joyeux Noël."

In German it is "Frohe Weihnachten."

In Russian it is "Christos Razdajetsja" (Христос рождается). This traditional Christmas greeting in Russian Orthodox communities means "Christ is born." The response to this greeting is "Slavite Jeho" (Славите Его), which means "Glorify Him."

In Gaelic, it is "Nollaig Shona Duit."

CHRISTMAS NAMES

The word **"Christmas"** is derived from "Christ's Mass," referring to the special liturgy celebrating the birth of Jesus Christ.

The words **"Noel," "Navidad,"** and **"Natale"** all come from the Latin "natalis," meaning "birth."

"Weihnachten" is the German word for Christmas.

"Nollaig" is the Irish Gaelic term for Christmas.

"Božić" is the name for Christmas in Croatian, Serbian, and other Slavic languages. Derived from the word "Bog," meaning "God," Božić literally means "little God," emphasizing the humility and innocence of the Christ child born on Christmas Day.

"Kerstmis" is the Dutch name for Christmas, with "Kerst" coming from "Christ" and "mis" meaning "Mass."

"Khristougenna" (Χριστούγεννα) is the Greek name for Christmas, meaning "Christ's Birth."

"Рождество" (**Rozhdestvo**) is the Russian word for Christmas, meaning "The Nativity."

CHRISTMAS ORNAMENTS

The Christmas tree was originally decorated with good things to eat: fruits, cookies, marzipan, candies wrapped in shiny foil, and even communion wafers! They were also decorated with things people made: eggs were blown out and decorated to look like angels or birds, and little animals and figures were made from straw.

In the 1800s, the German town of Lauscha was famous for its blown glass. The local glassworks was not doing well, and its workers were sinking into poverty. Many parents could not afford to decorate their Christmas trees with fruits, nuts, and candies. To avoid disappointing his children, a glassworks employee made glass ornaments in the shapes of fruit. His neighbors so admired them that they all began to make their own glass ornaments. Soon, the owner of the glassworks became interested and started producing them. The humble employee saved the factory and the people from bankruptcy.

Fifteen years later, at a store owned by Frank Woolworth, a traveling salesman appeared trying to sell glass ornaments he had imported from Lauscha. Woolworth didn't like them and only bought a few, but when his customers saw them, they loved them. Mr. Woolworth started importing them from Germany in huge numbers, as many as 200,000 a year!

CHRISTMAS TREE

Saint Boniface, an English missionary to Germany in the eighth century, is credited with creating the first authentic Christmas tree and firmly establishing the Church in German-speaking countries.

When Saint Boniface arrived in Germany, many pagan tribes worshiped trees. To show the tribes that trees had no power, he cut down a tree. He then brought the tree indoors, decorated it with lights, and taught the people to worship the true God who created the trees. He died a martyr's death and is now widely revered in Germany.

Traditionally, the Christmas Tree was not fully decorated until Christmas Eve and was decorated by the parents secretly. When the decorated Christmas tree was revealed to the children, it was with the understanding that the Christ Child decorated it.

During the 12 Days of Christmas, we leave the Christmas Tree up, fully decorated, to enjoy. It is not taken down until Epiphany or Candlemas.

CHRISTMAS WREATH

The Christmas Wreath, distinct from the Advent Wreath, is a tradition that dates back to the early North American colonists from England. These settlers brought their customs for celebrating the Twelve Days of Christmas, adapting and enriching them in their new homeland. Over time, they developed the tradition of the Christmas wreath made from greenery, ribbons, and fruits and hung on their front door.

Traditionally, these wreaths were made on Christmas Eve and displayed on each home's front door throughout the Twelve Days of Christmas, remaining in place until Twelfth Night or the morning of Epiphany. They are believed to be the origin of the modern-day Christmas wreath.

MANGER

The manger, central to the Nativity story, carries rich symbolism. As the humble place where Jesus was laid after His birth, the manger represents poverty and simplicity, highlighting how Christ, though divine, came into the world in a lowly and vulnerable state. This setting contrasts with worldly expectations of a king and underscores the humility of God's incarnation.

Additionally, the manger, a feeding trough for animals, symbolizes Jesus as the bread of life (John 6:35), born in Bethlehem, the Hebrew word that means "house of bread." Jesus is often compared to bread, which gives life and sustains believers.

In French, the word "manger" means "to eat," adding an interesting layer of symbolism to the manger. It's yet another connection to the theological concept of Christ as the "bread of life." It reinforces the idea of Christ coming into the world to be spiritually consumed—nourishing souls through His teachings, sacrifice, and presence in the Eucharist.

In the Eucharistic tradition, this symbolism is especially significant, as believers partake in Christ's body and blood, reflecting his role as the source of spiritual nourishment.

NATIVITY SCENE OR CRÈCHE

We're not done with the Nativity Scenes yet! On Christmas Eve, we will add baby Jesus to the manger, and as we move through the 12 Days of Christmas, we will move the Wise Men and camels closer to the manger until they finally arrive on Twelfth Night and Epiphany.

From the very first century of Christianity, pilgrimages were made to the site where Jesus was born in Bethlehem. An altar was built where the manger had been, and the Church of the Nativity was built over the site. Saint Francis of Assisi is credited with bringing the nativity scene into his hometown.

Saint Francis' nativity scene was created in Greccio, near Assisi, on Christmas Eve in 1223. It used real people and animals. The idea of a nativity scene in one's town quickly spread throughout Christendom. Shortly after, people began constructing large nativity scenes in their homes. The nativity scenes became smaller as the years passed and now fit on a table or shelf.

Traditionally, the nativity figures were set up in a certain way. Like an Advent Calendar, figures are slowly added to the scene. As Christmas Day approaches, Mary, Joseph, and the donkey move closer to the manger where the other animals are waiting. The shepherds and sheep also move closer until they finally arrive on Christmas Eve, when baby Jesus is also added to the manger. The Wise Men are the farthest away and move closer and closer until they finally arrive at the Feast of the Epiphany on January 6.

LIGHT

The Christ Child has come into this world! In the Gospel of John, we read, "In him was life, and that life was the light of all mankind. The light shines in the darkness, and the darkness has not overcome it" (John 1:4-5). Since light has always been a powerful symbol for Jesus, people worldwide use light to represent His birth during Christmas. Whether through lit candles, luminaries, or other forms of illumination, these lights serve as a reminder that Jesus is the Light of the World, shining in the darkness and bringing hope to all.

STOCKINGS

The traditional story associated with stockings involves Saint Nicholas. Legend has it that there was a poor man who had three daughters. The man had no money to get his daughters married, and he was worried about what would happen to them after his death. Saint Nicholas was passing through town when he heard the villagers talking about the girls, and he wanted to help. He knew that the old man would never accept charity, so he decided to help in secret. He waited until it was night and crept into the house with a bag of gold coins for each girl. While looking for a place to put three bags, he noticed stockings hung over the mantelpiece for drying. He put one bag in each stocking and left. When the girls and their father woke up the next morning, they found the bags of gold coins, and the girls were able to get married. This led to the custom of children hanging stockings or putting out shoes, eagerly awaiting gifts from Saint Nicholas on his feast day, December 6.

Although the stockings are traditionally filled on Saint Nicholas' Day, they are also traditionally filled on Christmas Eve.

THE PARADISE TREE

The Paradise Tree is a beautiful medieval tradition that predates and differs from the modern Christmas Tree. On Christmas Eve, a fir tree was adorned with dried apples, wafers, cookies, and pieces of candy. This tree was set up in both churches and private homes, serving as a symbolic reminder of humanity's fall and the promise of salvation.

The tradition of the Paradise Tree originates from the "Paradise Plays" of the Middle Ages, performed during Advent. These plays depicted Adam and Eve's fall in the Garden of Eden, their expulsion, and the prophecy of the coming Savior. The tree used in these plays represented Paradise, with the apples symbolizing the forbidden fruit and the wafers or bread representing the Eucharist, the Bread of Life. The sweets signified the sweetness of redemption through Christ.

In the 12th century, European Christians began celebrating the Feast of Saint Adam and Eve on Christmas Eve by reenacting the Genesis story with a Paradise Tree at the center of the stage. This practice, prevalent in Germany and France, eventually made its way to England, where Prince Albert, Queen Victoria's German husband, introduced the decorated Christmas tree to Buckingham Palace, continuing the symbolic tradition.

The Paradise Tree beautifully ties together the themes of humanity's fall and our redemption. As you decorate your Christmas tree this year, consider adding elements from the Paradise Tree tradition—like apples and wafers—to remind you of the significance of the Incarnation. The baubles on your tree can symbolize the apples from Eden, pointing to the reason for Christ's coming: the final victory over sin and death, opening the way to eternal life.

THE STAR OF BETHLEHEM

The Star of Bethlehem is a cherished symbol of the Christmas season, representing the heavenly light that guided the Wise Men to the birthplace of Jesus. Christians around the world use this symbol in their holiday decorations; whether it's atop the Christmas tree, on top of the home, hung from the windows, or as ornaments on the tree, the Star of Bethlehem serves as a reminder of the star that led the Magi to Christ.

YULE LOG

The Yule Log, also known as the Christmas Log, is a tradition rooted in the ancient winter celebrations of Europe and later adopted in North America. A large log was initially selected and brought into the home to be burned on the hearth during the Twelve Days of Christmas. The practice of burning the Yule Log dates back to at least the 17th century, with early references found in poetry and literature. As the log burned each night, it celebrated Christ's birth and symbolized the light of Christ entering the world and triumphing over sin and darkness.

The tradition called for burning a portion of the log each evening from Christmas Eve through Twelfth Night or Epiphany (the 12 Days of Christmas), with the remaining part saved to light the next year's log. This symbolized the continuity of life and the cyclical nature of the seasons of the Church.

The Bûche de Noël

The Yule Log tradition has also inspired a delightful culinary adaptation, the Bûche de Noël, or Yule Log cake. This dessert originated in France in the 19th century and is made from a rolled sponge cake filled with buttercream and frosted to resemble a log. The cake's design, often with textured "bark" and decorations like meringue mushrooms, pays homage to the original Yule Log. While the practice of burning a Yule Log has faded in some areas, the Bûche de Noël remains a popular Christmas treat, symbolizing the warmth and festivity of the season in a deliciously modern form.

CHRISTMAS TRADITIONS FOR SPECIFIC DAYS

There are many traditional ways to observe Christmastide and all of the special days that fall within it. All of the following things are given as aids to focus our attention and to mark the passage of the holy season. Choose as many as you like, but don't overwhelm yourself or your family with too many. They are given to enrich our lives, not to burden us. After choosing some, incorporate them into your daily and weekly devotions.

In addition to the overall season of Christmastide, there are special days to celebrate, such as feast days, where we remember special people in the Church's life. Find the dates according to the year and mark them in your calendar. You can always find a current Liturgical Calendar with all of these dates on my website:

www.AshleyTumlinWallace.com

A note about feast days in the church - they always start at sundown the day before.

CHRISTMAS EVE (DECEMBER 24)

The liturgical color for Christmas Eve is white or gold, symbolizing a high, holy day.

Today, you will know that the Lord is coming to save us, and in the morning, you will see his Glory!

On Christmas Eve, we are suspended between two worlds —the world of darkness, sin, and death and the new world of light promised through God's Messiah. On this day, the season of Advent draws to an end, and the waiting and intentional preparation come to a close. Christmas Eve is our last opportunity to heed Saint John the Baptist's words to "prepare the way of the Lord." This is why, traditionally, Christmas Eve is a day for confession.

Although we continue to prepare our hearts through confession and introspection, it's hard to contain our excitement because we know what happens at the stroke of midnight—the dawn of a new age arrives with the birth of a Savior who will ransom us from sin and death and bring us back to our loving Father!

Christmas Day is one of the highest feast days of the Christian Year, the culmination of all that Advent has been preparing us for. Christmas Eve is a day of great anticipation and preparation, an excellent opportunity to cultivate a sense of wonder and joy within your family, centered on the birth of the Christ Child. If possible, make this a very special family day where everyone is together, watching, waiting, and preparing as one. Encourage your children to participate in all of these activities to create a sense of excitement and anticipation. Christmas Eve is the final day of preparation for the Christmas Feast—use this time to prepare not only your home, food, and clothes but also your hearts for the joy that is to come.

Remember, there are many different traditions and ways to celebrate—choose what suits your family. There is no one right way as long as Jesus is glorified.

Ways to Celebrate

In the Morning

Traditionally, on the morning of December 24, most Christmas Day preparations have been completed. All cookies and treats made for the Christmas feast are hidden away. The kitchen looks sober and bare compared to the night before, with nothing left out but the makings of a very simple breakfast and lunch. This is so counter to how we celebrate now, but Christmas Eve was one of the strictest fast days of the Christian year. All over the world, many people consume no more than a cup of coffee and a piece of bread for breakfast, and lunch is usually water and a small meatless meal. With these frugal meals, the holy season of Advent draws to a close.

Many beautiful traditions surround the Christmas tree, and families worldwide celebrate in different ways.

In the United States, putting up the Christmas tree at the beginning of Advent is common. If your tree is already up, Christmas Eve is a beautiful time to gather around it with your family.

However, the Christmas tree isn't put up in many other parts of the world until Christmas Eve afternoon. Some families enjoy decorating the tree together, making it a shared experience that builds excitement for the night ahead. In other traditions, parents secretly decorate the tree, and the fully decorated tree is revealed to the children later on Christmas Eve or Christmas morning. This moment is often filled with wonder, as the children understand that the Christ Child has blessed them with both the gifts and the decorations.

To create a sense of mystery and anticipation, consider closing off the room where the tree and presents will be revealed. If you don't have a door, cover the entrance with a sheet or wrapping paper and add a handwritten sign that says "Top Secret" or "Keep Out." Let the children know that this is where the Christ Child will bless them with gifts and a fully decorated tree and that no one is allowed to enter the room until the right moment. This simple act can add to the magic of Christmas Eve and make the experience even more special.

Clean house! As a final act of preparation, it is an Irish and Eastern European tradition to clean your house, return all borrowed items, and fix everything in your home that needs to be repaired.

Lunch

Make a simple lunch. In many Christian traditions, particularly among those observing a more solemn Advent or preparing for a larger meal later on Christmas Eve, lunch on Christmas Eve is often kept simple and light. This usually includes simple soups, salads, and snack boards, allowing people to save their appetite for the more elaborate evening feasts.

In the Afternoon

In the afternoon, in many countries around the world, it's time to decorate the Christmas tree—a special moment filled with anticipation for the night ahead. If you haven't already decorated your Christmas tree, you have two beautiful options, depending on how your family would like to celebrate.

Option 1: Decorate Together as a Family

Gather the family around and make decorating the tree a shared experience. Begin by turning on Handel's Messiah to create a joyful and reverent atmosphere. Let everyone participate—hang the ornaments, string the lights, and place the star or angel on top. As you work together, share stories of past Christmases, discuss the meaning of each ornament, or reflect on the day's significance. This togetherness deepens the anticipation and joy for the evening ahead.

Once the tree is fully decorated, take a moment to refresh the Advent wreath and place the presents under the tree. Set the dining table for the Christmas feast, arranging the cookies and foods you've prepared in advance. Place the Christmas crib by the tree, with a bell next to the Nativity scene, as a reminder of the coming holy night. If you've been using a Jesse Tree, gather the family to hang the final ornament together, completing this meaningful tradition as a family.

Option 2: Decorate in Secret

If you prefer to surprise the children with a fully decorated tree, create a special activity for them. Send them to their rooms for some quiet time, placing special Advent and Christmas books on their pillows—books you've collected and saved just for this occasion. Alternatively, a loved one or relative could take the children outside to play or visit other family members, giving you the space to prepare.

While the children are occupied, take this opportunity to reflect on the birth of Christ, relax, and embrace the significance of the day. With Handel's *Messiah* playing in the background, bring in the Christmas tree and fully decorate it. Refresh the Advent wreath, place the presents under the tree, and set the dining table for the Christmas feast. Arrange the cookies and foods you've prepared in advance, ready to be enjoyed. Place the Christmas crib by the tree, with a bell next to the Nativity scene, adding a touch of anticipation for the night ahead. If you've been using a Jesse Tree, hang the final ornament to complete this cherished tradition.

Listen to the Nine Lessons and Carols, broadcast by the BBC annually from King's College, Cambridge, on Christmas Eve. The service has established itself as one of the major signs that Christmas has begun in the United Kingdom.

Take extra care of animals. Aside from Joseph and Mary, the animals in the manger were the first witnesses of the Messiah's birth. Before the shepherds arrived, the animals looked on with wonder as the Redeemer of the world lay in a manger. Because they were the very first witnesses, legend has it that God honored the animals by allowing them to speak. The rooster yelled, "Christ is born!" The cow asked, "Where?" The sheep answered, "Bethlehem." "Let's go!" said the donkey. There is also a legend that cattle kneel at midnight on Christmas Eve to honor the Savior's birth.

Because the animals were present at the birth of Christ and because it was such a momentous occasion, Saint Francis urged that all animals be fed extra portions on Christmas Eve to include them in the celebration. That's why it has long been a tradition to provide additional food for animals on this night. Decorate the trees in the yard with popcorn garlands and birdseed, and put out extra portions of food for your animals. You could also make chickadee pudding for the birds. The recipe is found in the recipe section of the book.

In the Evening

The evening marks the beginning of the Christmas festivities leading into Christmas Day. In countries around the world, this time has special names. In Germany, it is known as *Heiligabend*, or "Holy Evening," while in Spanish-speaking countries, it is called *Noche Buena*, or "Good Night." During this time, families and friends gather for a festive meal and to exchange gifts. After these celebrations, they attend the Christmas Eve Vigil and return home for an extravagant party and meal.

Light candles. Since light has always been a symbol of Jesus, people worldwide use light to represent the birth of Jesus.

In the southwestern United States, entire neighborhoods line their streets and walkways with luminaries on Christmas Eve and Christmas Day. In many Irish families, candles wreathed in holly are lit in every window on Christmas Eve. In Ireland, the Great Christmas candle is lit and is big enough to last all twelve days of Christmas. Each family member lights a smaller candle from the large one. The family then prays and exchanges blessings. A three-pronged candelabra is lit in France and England, representing the Trinity. Slavic and Ukrainian families keep a large Christ candle in the center of their dining table.

The Christmas Eve Meal Before the Vigil

The Christmas Eve meal is the final moment of Advent, one of the most significant and sacred meals of the Christian year, and is lovingly referred to as the "Holy Meal." It is a time when families and friends reaffirm their bonds of love and unity in Christ. Like Christmas Eve, this meal is filled with joyful expectancy and is deeply celebratory, yet it often includes a sense of fasting within the feast. Traditionally, meat is abstained from, reflecting a jubilant abstinence.

The meal before the Vigil carries beautiful food traditions centered around a meatless dish and lavish desserts. Every detail is rich with meaning. In many countries, the meal begins when the first star appears in the sky, symbolizing the Star of Bethlehem. The table is often candlelit, with a large white candle in the center representing Christ as the Light of the World. Bread plays a significant role in the meal, symbolizing Christ as the Bread of Life. Additionally, the courses and desserts are often numbered, each holding spiritual significance.

In Slavic countries, the floor and dining table are strewn with straw in honor of the stable where Jesus was born. A white tablecloth representing the swaddling clothes that wrapped the infant Jesus is placed over the dining table's straw.

The meal begins with the breaking of the Christmas Wafer, a thin, unleavened wafer made from flour and water, similar in composition to the communion wafers used during communion. The wafers are made in an iron mold and stamped with scenes of the Nativity. The head of the household breaks the wafer, shares it with each family member, and wishes them a blessed Christmas.

In Poland, the Christmas Eve meal is called *Wigilia*, from the Latin word *vigilare*, meaning "to be on watch," since this is the night we eagerly await the birth of Christ. The Christmas wafer, known as Oplatek, comes from the Latin word *oblatum*, meaning "offering" or "gift." In the late 18th century, when Poland lost its independence and was divided among three empires, families and friends were often separated. Polish Christians would send Oplatek in letters during the Christmas season to keep their traditions alive and maintain a sense of connection. This gesture symbolized comfort and the enduring bond that no distance could break.

In Italy, the meal is known as The Feast of the Seven Fishes, which represents Mary's seven sorrows. In southern France, it is called Le Gros Souper, or "Great Supper," and also features seven dishes. Le Gros Souper is followed by 13 desserts symbolizing Christ and the 12 apostles. The 13 desserts are usually dried fruit and nuts, quince paste, biscotti, nougat, pain d'épices (spiced bread), and other small delicacies.

Before the Vigil

After the meal, many Christians around the world exchange gifts and then leave for the Christmas Eve Vigil.

In many Spanish-speaking countries, people light fireworks before heading to the Vigil. In Caracas, Venezuela, the streets are closed downtown so people can go to the Vigil on rollerblades and roller skates!

The Christmas Eve Vigil or Midnight Mass

Next to Jesus' death and resurrection, the celebration of his birth is one of the most important days in the Christian year. On this holy night, joining with the faithful worldwide, we gather in joy and anticipation to welcome the arrival of our Savior.

The Christmas Eve Vigil, also known as Midnight Mass, is an ancient liturgy with roots dating back to the early centuries of the Church. By the 4th century, December 25th had been formally established as the date to celebrate the Nativity of Christ, and the tradition of holding a vigil on Christmas Eve became widespread. This holy night is the culmination of Advent, the season of preparation, and marks the first true celebration of Christmas.

Traditionally, the service begins late in the evening and continues until just after midnight so that the Eucharist is celebrated as Christmas Day begins. On this most holy night, our Lord Jesus Christ was born, and we, as the Church, gather to remember and rejoice in this glorious mystery. We hear the wondrous story of Christ's birth again, joining with the shepherds who first heard the good news from the angels. In many traditions, the vigil is called the "Shepherds' Mass" (Missa Pastoralis), honoring those humble shepherds who were the first to adore the newborn Savior.

In Spanish-speaking countries, this liturgy is known as Misa de Gallo, or the "Rooster's Mass," a beautiful image of the rooster heralding the dawn of salvation. Just as the rooster crows to announce the morning, we gather to proclaim the coming of the Light of the World, Jesus Christ.

As the service begins, the church is transformed and adorned with candles and wreaths, and the Nativity scene is created, creating a warm, sacred atmosphere filled with anticipation. After a long season of waiting through Advent, the first Christmas carol is finally sung, often a cherished hymn such as "O Come, All Ye Faithful" or "Once in Royal David's City."

The liturgy includes readings from both the Old and New Testaments, with the Gospel of Luke taking center stage, telling the beloved story of the Nativity. In some churches, this reading is accompanied by a dramatic procession, re-enacting the journey of Mary and Joseph to Bethlehem or the angels announcing Christ's birth to the shepherds.

At the heart of the Christmas Eve Vigil is the celebration of the Eucharist. In this most sacred act, we give thanks for the Incarnation—the Word made flesh. Christ, the Bread of Heaven, was born so that he might be broken and given for us. As we partake of the Body and Blood of our Savior, we are reminded of the great love that God has shown us in sending his Son into the world to redeem us.

One of the most moving moments of the service comes after Communion, when the church falls into a peaceful stillness. The congregation is given candles, and the only light in the darkened sanctuary comes from their glow, symbolizing the light of Christ entering the world. Together, we sing "Silent Night," a hymn that captures the quiet reverence of the moment. The gentle flicker of the candles, combined with the soft melody of the carol, invites us to contemplate the miracle of the Nativity in a spirit of awe and wonder.

As the service draws to a close, a passage from the Gospel of John (1:1-14) is often read: "In the beginning was the Word, and the Word was with God, and the Word was God." These powerful words remind us of the eternal significance of Christ's birth. Then, suddenly, the lights are turned on, flooding the church with brightness as the congregation bursts into a triumphant hymn such as "Joy to the World" or "Hark! The Herald Angels Sing." The joy of the Incarnation fills the space as we leave, carrying with us the light and hope of Christ into the night.

This sacred vigil not only marks the beginning of Christmas but also draws us deeper into the mystery of our faith. On this holy night, heaven touches earth, and we celebrate that God is with us. The joy and reverence of the service linger long after we depart, a reminder that the light of Christ continues to shine in our hearts and in the world.

So, this Christmas Eve, attend the Vigil at your church. Sing the carols, receive the Eucharist, and rejoice in the birth of our Savior. For on this night, we welcome the Light of the World, and through Him, we receive grace upon grace.

If attending the Christmas Eve service is not possible, gather around your Advent wreath, do the devotion, and light the Christ candle.

After the devotion, move into the room with the decorated tree. We are now moving from Advent into Christmas! This is the time to joyfully sing your first Christmas carol! Go through the darkened house, singing, until you see the living room with the entryway open and light flooding out of the room. The children will walk into a room with candles lit, the tree fully decorated, music playing, and presents laid out. What a magical scene! What a stark contrast to go from the light of the Advent wreath to a room blazing with light and music.

Wish everyone a very blessed Christmas, and place your baby Jesus figurine in the manger.

The Meal After the Vigil

Following the Christmas Eve Vigil, many Christians around the world celebrate with a grand and festive meal. This elaborate feast, which often begins late at night, fully ushers in the joy of Christmas Day.

In France, it is known as Réveillon. The word *réveillon* comes from the French *réveil*, meaning "awakening," symbolizing how the light of Christ has broken into our lives, awakening us from darkness.

Réveillon is a multi-course feast that often includes indulgent dishes such as foie gras, oysters, roasted meats, and Bûche de Noël, a Yule log-shaped cake that symbolizes the Light of Christ coming into the world. Every course is a proclamation of God's goodness, lavishly poured out in the Incarnation. The meal is rich, joyful, and celebratory, a marked contrast to the fasting and simplicity of the Advent season. (The recipe for the Bûche de Noël can be found in the book's recipe section.)

In Austria and Germany, the focus is often on special Christmas breads, like Stollen, filled with fruits and nuts, and a festive punch to toast the joyous occasion. These delicacies are enjoyed in the warm glow of Christmas lights as families gather late into the night, rejoicing in the birth of the Savior. (The recipe for Stollen can be found in the book's recipe section.)

In many Latin American countries, the Christmas Eve feast is called *Noche Buena*, meaning "Good Night." After the Misa de Gallo, families gather for a late-night meal that continues the celebration of Christ's birth. Tables are filled with traditional dishes like tamales, bacalao, and roast pork, each representing the region's flavors and heritage. Gifts are exchanged, and the celebrations spill over into the early hours of Christmas Day as loved ones come together to share the season's food, laughter, and joy.

In many places, the night is further marked by fireworks, the ringing of church bells, and neighbors stepping outside to wish each other a Merry Christmas. It is a night of festivity, community, and the deep joy of knowing that the long-awaited Savior has come.

Whether enjoyed in the quiet warmth of candlelight or in the jubilant celebrations with friends and neighbors, this post-Vigil meal invites us to continue feasting on the goodness of God. As we gather around the table, we remember that Christ, the Bread of Life, has come to dwell among us, and through Him, we are filled with hope, joy, and love. The Christmas feast—whether a simple midnight supper or an extravagant Réveillon— proclaims the glory of the newborn King and the abundant life He brings to all.

THE FEAST OF THE NATIVITY, CHRISTMAS DAY (DECEMBER 25)

> Joy to the World!
> The Lord has come!
> Let Earth receive her King!

The birth of our long-awaited Savior has finally come! Christmas Day is a feast day of the highest order. It is the day of days that celebrates the mystery of the Incarnation.

The God of the universe humbled himself, took on flesh, and walked among us. Finally, we are able to celebrate the long-awaited birth of Christ with Christians all over the world!

As we celebrate, we remember with joy the message of the angels, "Glory to God in the highest, and on earth peace, goodwill towards men" (Luke 2:14). It is with these words that we see the loving hand of God. God has sent to us a Savior, his very son, Jesus, to redeem us, to set us free, and to bring us back to himself. What a glorious day this is!

Ways to Celebrate Christmas Day

It is traditional to greet each other with a kiss and the words: "Christ is Born!" to which the one being greeted responds: "Glorify Him!"

If you've waited until Christmas morning to open your gifts, open Christmas gifts!

Attend Christmas Day services at your church or do the devotion for the day.

Sing Christmas carols! This is the time to sing them to yourself and your family. Go over the words and think about what they say and mean in your life.

This is also a day to remember and include the lonely and those who have recently lost loved ones.

If you have a nativity scene, start moving the three kings (placed some distance away) closer to the manger. Time the movement of the kings to last until the Feast of the Epiphany on January 6.

In Creole Louisiana, Christmas Day is marked by a grand feast, beginning with a hearty breakfast. A typical morning meal might include sliced oranges, hominy, steak and potatoes, omelets, and rice cakes drizzled with cane syrup, all accompanied by café au lait. (The recipe for Rice Cakes with Louisiana Syrup is in the recipe section.)

In Italy, there is technically no formal Christmas Day dinner. Instead, the most significant meal of *Natale* (Christmas) is a leisurely lunch that can last for hours. Unlike Christmas Eve's seafood-focused feast, Christmas Day is a celebration filled with rich, meat-based dishes. The meal begins with a traditional *antipasto* spread featuring dry-cured meats like salumi, fine Italian cheeses, briny olives, artichokes, and more. The first course is pasta, though the type varies by region. In Southern and Central Italy, baked pasta is a staple, while favorites like lasagne Bolognese, manicotti, or ravioli are served in the North. The star of the meal is the main course, which may include roasted veal, baked chicken, sausages, or braised beef—delicacies worthy of the festive season.

In some countries, Christmas Day is a time for a lavish and joyful feast, a chance to serve your finest dishes in celebration of the birth of our Savior. Roast goose is served in many countries, such as Great Britain, the United States, and Germany. A recipe for Roast Goose is in the recipe section.

In Germany, they serve Knodel and Red Cabbage along with the Goose.

In England, it is the day to bring out the cherished Christmas plum pudding. Plum pudding, or Christmas pudding, is a beloved tradition, often presented with a flourish. After the main meal, the pudding is brought to the table, soaked in brandy or another festive spirit, and set alight. This dramatic moment, with its dancing flames, fills the room with warmth and reminds us of the season's joy. To serve the pudding, the lights are dimmed, and the flaming dessert is carried to the table. Once the flames subside, it is shared among the family, brimming with rich ingredients that symbolize the abundance Christ brings on His birthday. A recipe for Plum Pudding is found in the book's recipe section.

The family gathers for a devotion and carol singing in the Christmas room after the feast. As you settle into this peaceful moment, offer something warm to drink, like a French-style hot chocolate or a spiced cider, to keep the festive spirit alive. Eat Stollen and coffee.

THE FEAST OF SAINT STEPHEN (DECEMBER 26)

On the Feast of Saint Stephen, the church celebrates the very first martyr to die because of his love for Jesus. You can find Saint Stephen's story in the Book of Acts. The apostles elected Stephen to take care of the needs of the poor in their community so that the apostles could focus on preaching and teaching God's Word. Tradition tells us that Stephen was full of grace and fortitude and did great wonders and signs among the people. One day, while Stephen was preaching the Gospel in the streets, angry Jews, who believed his message about Jesus to be blasphemy, dragged him outside of the city and stoned him to death. Since Saint Stephen was the first Christian martyr, the church gave his day of remembrance a special place of honor on the day immediately after we celebrate Christ's birth.

Ways to Celebrate

In many countries around the world, Saint Stephen's Day is a holiday. It is a day to visit family and friends or to take a long walk in the countryside. In Italy, they play board games and cards; in Poland, they jump into an icy body of water; and in Australia, they go to the beach to swim.

Give your alms to the poor. Since Saint Stephen's role in the Christian community was to care for those in need, Christians used this day to distribute the alms boxes they collected during Advent to those in need.

In England, small gifts of money are given to those who provide services during the year. These gifts of money were called "boxes." Thus, Saint Stephen's Day became known as "Boxing Day."

The origin of the piggy bank also comes from this day. Children in Germany and Holland stored their money in pig-shaped earthenware containers, which they then broke on Saint Stephen's Day. The money saved was distributed to the poor.

Throw rice at each other. In Poland, people give Saint Stephen's Day "blessings" by throwing handfuls of rice, oats, or walnuts at one another. The act symbolizes the stoning of Saint Stephen!

Make Saint Stephen's Horseshoes. The origins are unclear, but Saint Stephen became the patron saint of horses. On this day, in Poland and other Eastern European countries, bread is baked in the shape of horseshoes. (The recipe can be found in the recipe section of the book)

Make Bubble and Squeak and Mulled Ale. In England, the traditional fare for Saint Stephen's Day is a roasted vegetable dish known as "Bubble and Squeak" and Mulled Ale. Recipes for each of these items can be found in the book's recipe section.

Eat leftovers. Saint Stephen's Day in Italy is also called *il giorno degli avanzi*, "the day of the leftovers." All of the leftover food from the Christmas Eve and Christmas Day feasts is reworked and enjoyed for lunch. Have a leftover poultry carcass? Make *passatelli in brodo*. A thick dough made of cheese, breadcrumbs, and egg yolks is pressed through a special sieve-like implement to form golden noodles, which are cooked in the broth and served piping hot. The recipe can be found in the recipe section of the book.

THE FEAST OF SAINT JOHN (DECEMBER 27)

Saint John was a simple fisherman from Galilee. Along with his brother James, John became a faithful disciple of Christ. He is the only apostle who was at the cross when Jesus died. While at the cross, Jesus asked him to take care of Mary. He is believed to be the writer of the gospel of John, the Letters of John, and the Book of Revelation.

Legend has it that he traveled with Peter in Judea and then went on to Asia Minor, where he founded the seven churches mentioned in Revelation. Saint John faithfully preached the gospel for the rest of his life and was eventually exiled to the island of Patmos. He is the only disciple who did not suffer a martyr's fate.

A central theme of Saint John's ministry and writings is the love of Christ. He writes in 1 John that "God is love, and all who live in love live in God." He always refers to himself as the "beloved disciple," and Saint Jerome wrote that every time Saint John was asked to preach, he would stand before the crowd and say, "Love one another. This is the Lord's command." What a profound and simple message!

Ways to Celebrate

Drink from the Saint John's Cup. Legend has it that Saint John's enemies presented him with a cup of poisoned wine. Before Saint John drank from the cup, he made the sign of the cross. Immediately, the cup split, the poisoned wine spilled out, and Saint John was saved.

In memory of this event, people brought their house wine to the church, and the priest blessed it. That night, the family would gather for dinner, and everyone would be given a glass of the blessed wine. The father would begin the celebration by having everyone stand with their glass of wine. He would touch his glass to his wife's glass, look her in the eye, and say, "I drink to you the love of Saint John." The mother would then reply, "I thank you for the love of Saint John," and they both would take a sip of wine.

The mother would then turn to the oldest child and say, "I drink to you the love of Saint John." The oldest child would then answer, "I thank you for the love of Saint John," and they would both take a sip of wine. The oldest child then turned to the next oldest child, and the pattern was repeated until the youngest child faced the father, repeated the phrase, and closed the family circle.

The remaining wine would be stored away and used when a family member was sick (1 Timothy 5:23) or a time of grand celebration. Also, if a family member was about to take a trip, a few drops of the blessed wine were added to each wine glass, and the whole family would drink "the love of Saint John" again. Immediately after the wedding ceremony, the newlywed couple also drank the love of Saint John with each other.

Celebrate the day by making your own Saint John's Wine (the recipe is in the book's recipe section) and having your own Saint John's Cup Ceremony.

◡

A Blessing For the St. John's Wine

Light the Christ candle. Begin your devotion time with the following invitation to prayer:

Leader: Our help is in the name of the Lord.
People: **Who has made heaven and earth.**
Leader: The Lord be with you.
All: **And with your spirit.**

Leader: Let us pray. Lord, we pray that you would bless and consecrate this cup of wine, and every drink. We pray that all who believe in you and drink of this cup may be blessed and protected. Blessed John drank poison from the cup, and was in no way harmed. So, too, may all who this day drink from this cup in honor of Blessed John, be freed from every sickness and harm.
People: **Amen.**

Leader: Bless, O Lord, this wine which you have made. May it be a healthful refreshment to all who drink of it. And grant by the invocation of your holy name that whoever tastes of it may, by your generosity, receive health of both soul and body, through Christ our Lord.
People: **Amen.**

THE FEAST OF THE HOLY INNOCENTS (DECEMBER 28)

The Feast of the Holy Innocents is the commemoration of all of the male children who were killed under the rule of King Herod. The feast has been celebrated since 485 AD; the account can be found in the Gospel of Matthew.

In the Gospel of Matthew, we are told that the Wise Men went to King Herod seeking the "one who had been born king of the Jews." Herod was greatly troubled by this news but assembled the chief priests and teachers of the law to tell them where this child could be. They answered that the child would be found in Bethlehem. Herod called the Wise Men to him and gave them the location. He asked that as soon as they found the child, they would report back to him so that he might come and worship him as well.

The Wise Men found the Christ Child and worshipped him. They offered him gifts worthy of a king. As they started on their journey to return to King Herod, they were warned in a dream not to return to him, so they returned to their homeland by another route.

When Herod realized that the Wise Men had outwitted him, he was furious. To keep this infant king from one day growing up to take his throne, He gave orders for all of the boys two years and under to be killed in Bethlehem and its vicinity. These infants became known in the Church as the Holy Innocents. The day is also known as

Childermas or Children's Mass because it is when the Church blesses children in a special "Children's Mass." This day is also a special day to remember those children who are suffering around the world.

Ways to Celebrate

Allow your children to rule for the day. In medieval monastery schools, it was traditional to elect one boy from among the students to be ruler for the day. The boy was allowed to run the monastery for the entire day. He decided what foods to eat, what they would do for the day, etc. The tradition spread to families and continues to this day. The youngest children of the family are given the rule of the house and get to make all of the decisions.

Play pranks on each other. It is a day for pranks in Spain, Central and South America, and the Philippines. These pranks are known as *inocentadas*, and their victims are called *inocentes*. The rule for the day is that there can be no punishments for the pranks pulled, and no one can get angry about them!

Venezuelans call it *Fiesta de Locos* or "Feast of Fools" because Herod must have been crazy to order the murder of innocent children.

If you're really brave, let your children have a flour fight! In Ibi, Spain, they hold a festival where the "innocents" dress up and incite a flour fight.

Listen to the Coventry Carol. The carol originated in Coventry, England, where it was performed as part of a mystery play called *The Pageant of the Shearmen and Tailors.* The play tells the Christmas story found in Matthew 2. The carol is about the Massacre of the Innocents and is a lullaby of the mothers to their doomed children.

Pray for the children who are suffering around the world.

NEW YEAR'S EVE OR SAINT SYLVESTER'S DAY (DECEMBER 31ST)

In many countries, December 31st is considered the last day of the calendar year. Traditionally, it begins as a day of strict fasting, abstinence, and confession to emphasize the day's seriousness and thoughtfulness. Another year is over, and a new one is about to begin. This is an appropriate time to look back over the entire year and reflect on all the good and bad things. It is a time to thank God for all of the good and to also thank him for how he redeemed or is redeeming the bad.

It is also the Eve of Saint Sylvester's Day. According to medieval legend, Saint Sylvester was responsible for the conversion and baptism of Constantine the Great, the Roman Emperor, who ended the long persecution of Christians. Constantine ushered in a new era of freedom and peace for Christians, and Saint Sylvester is celebrated for it.

Ways to Celebrate

Make Saint Sylvester's Punch and Krapfen. In Austria, when the clock strikes twelve on New Year's Eve, people eat krapfen, or apricot jam doughnuts, and drink Saint Sylvester's Punch. The recipes are in the book's recipe section.

It is traditional in many European countries for the father to bless everyone in the family and for the children to offer thanks to their parents for all of their love and care.

Do the devotion for the day. Hold your own service for New Year's Eve in your home, where you can thank God for the blessings of the past year and seek blessings for the year to come. Commend the previous and next year to God's mercies and ask that they be sanctified with our Lord's blessing.

Eat 12 grapes. In Spain and Italy, a grape is eaten at each of the 12 chimes of the clock at midnight to welcome the New Year and honor the 12 disciples.

THE FEAST OF THE HOLY NAME OR NEW YEAR'S DAY (JANUARY 1ST)

New Year's Day is a day for festivities and merrymaking. In the Church, it is also the Feast of the Holy Name of Jesus. This is the day that the Church remembers the naming and circumcision of Jesus.

It was a Jewish custom for newborn boys to be named and circumcised eight days after they were born. This is why the feast occurs eight days after Christmas Day.

And when eight days were completed for the circumcision of the Child, his name was called Jesus, the name given by the angel before he was conceived in the womb.

Luke 2:21

The name "Jesus," meaning "God saves," emphasizes his pivotal role in human salvation. Invoking the name of Jesus is central to our prayers and worship because we, as Christians, believe in the power of his holy name.

Therefore, God exalted him to the highest place and gave him the name that is above every name, that at the name of Jesus, every knee should bow, in heaven and on earth and under the earth, and every tongue acknowledge that Jesus Christ is Lord, to the glory of God the Father.

Philippians 2:9-11

Ways to Celebrate

In Coventry, England, it is traditional to visit your godchild on this day and bring them "God-cakes." God Cakes are little triangular cakes (in honor of the Trinity) with sweet filling. The recipe can be found in the recipe section of the book.

Wear white. In Brazil, Christians dress in white, symbolizing forgiveness of sins for the previous year and the purity of a new year and new life in Christ.

Wake up early. In Switzerland, on the morning of Saint Sylvester's Day, the children compete with one another to see who can wake up the earliest; the child who wakes up the latest is playfully teased.

For centuries, huge festivals have been held in regions of Switzerland. Men masquerade as Silvesterklaus, a masked person in an elaborate costume, taking part in Saint Sylvester's Day festivities. In Appenzell, Switzerland, the Silvesterkläuse put on their strange costumes, rang huge bells, sang a very slow yodel, and walked in small groups from house to house, wishing people a happy new year.

TWELFTH NIGHT (JANUARY 5TH)

The celebration of Twelfth Night and Epiphany is one of the oldest celebrations in the church—it is even older than the celebration of Christmas Day! The celebration originated in Egypt in the 3rd century and is the last vestige of an ancient Christian celebration called Smoke Nights. Every night, beginning on Christmas Eve and lasting for twelve nights, Christians celebrated these nights by going through their homes and barns, burning incense, and blessing their homesteads. Only one of these nights is left now, which is called Twelfth Night.

Twelfth Night, or Eve of the Epiphany, begins at sundown and is the beginning of the Epiphany celebration. On this day, we celebrate the wise men's long journey and their meeting with the child Jesus.

In the Gospel of Matthew, we are told that wise men came from the east to Jerusalem, looking for the one born to be the King of the Jews. They were led by a bright and unusual star in the sky that they knew signified the birth of a mighty king. They brought gifts worthy of a king and traveled for quite some time until they arrived at King Herod's palace seeking the "one who had been born king of the Jews." Herod was greatly troubled by what the Wise Men said. He assembled the chief priests and teachers of the law to tell them where this child would be. They searched the scriptures and answered that the child would be found in Bethlehem.

Herod called the Wise Men to him and gave them the location. He asked that as soon as they found the child, they would report back to him so that he might come and worship him as well.

The Wise Men were led to a humble home where Jesus lived with Mary and Joseph. When they arrived, they rejoiced with "exceedingly great joy." They entered the house, saw the young child, fell down, and worshipped him. Then, they presented the child with their treasures: gold, frankincense, and myrrh.

The church recognizes this beautiful moment as an epiphany. An epiphany is a sudden revelation that reveals something's true nature or meaning. At this moment, God's plan for salvation through Jesus was revealed to the world beyond the Jews. Through the Wise Men's visit, we see that through Jesus, God's plan of salvation is meant for everyone.

Although Twelfth Night and Epiphany are not celebrated much in the United States, they are major holidays in other countries. There is feasting and parades through the streets. Men dressed as Wise Men can be seen parading down the streets, and Wise Men figures are placed at town nativity scenes. This is the last great feast in the Christmas cycle and is wonderfully celebrated.

Ways to Celebrate

Do the devotion for the evening.

Bless Your Home. After the evening meal, it is traditional in many countries for the family to follow the father through the house and farm. The father goes from room to room, burning incense. He is followed by another member of the family who carries a bowl filled with holy water and sprinkles the holy water freely throughout every room of the house.

The rest of the family, holding a star affixed to a branch or pole and figures of the Wise Men, process behind them to the Nativity creche. They sing hymns to mark the event, such as "We Three Kings of Orient Are."

They then make their way to the last room of the house, where the nativity scene is. They place the kings around baby Jesus, lying in the manger. After the adoration of baby Jesus, the family writes the initials C, M, and B in chalk above their front door. The initials stand for the names traditionally given to the wise men: Caspar, Melchior, and Balthasar, and also for "Christ, bless this house" in Latin (*Christus mansionem benedicat*). The initials are then surrounded by the current year and separated by crosses (20+C+M+B+24).

Sing Door to Door. On Twelfth Night, Christians around the world go door to door in their neighborhoods and sing carols. The carol singers go from house to house singing and wishing their neighbors good health. In Great Britain, it is known as wassailing.

In Austria and Germany, "Star Singers" visit houses. They are led by a person carrying a large star hanging from a pole or stick. They represent the three Wise Men and carry decorated boxes representing the gifts the Wise Men gave to Jesus. They collect money, which they give to the poor.

Drink something sweet and warm. In Great Britain, while wassailing, special warm and sweet drinks called Wassail and Lamb's Wool are served. In Mexico, they drink hot chocolate or atole (a warm, thick, grain-based drink). The recipes are found in the recipe section of the book.

Make a special cake. All over the world, Christians also make a simple cake with a dried bean inside for Twelfth

Night. Whoever finds the bean in their cake is crowned king or queen for the night and might also have duties assigned to them at a later celebration. In Great Britain, it is The Twelfth Night Cake; in the United States, it is called King Cake; in France, it is called Galette de Rois; and in Spanish-speaking countries, it is known as the Rosca de Reyes. There are special traditions with whoever finds the baby Jesus figurine or the bean. In some countries, you are expected to host a party on Candlemas, celebrated on February 2nd; in others, you become the queen or king for the day.

Give gifts. In many countries, children believe that the Magi come to them and bring gifts just as they did to Jesus on Epiphany. In the days leading up to Epiphany or Three Kings' Day, children write letters to the three kings asking for a toy or gift. The children leave their shoes out the night before Epiphany. They add some hay to their shoes for the camels to eat. When the children wake up in the morning, gifts appear in their shoes in place of the hay. Have your children leave out their shoes before bed and fill them with little toys or candy while they sleep.

Light your Christmas Log or Yule Log. This is the final night to light your Christmas Log or Yule Log.

Burn your Christmas tree. Traditionally, Christians worldwide save their Christmas trees until Twelfth Night or Candlemas, when they gather around them and burn them.

THE FEAST OF THE EPIPHANY (JANUARY 6TH)

Epiphany, also known as Three Kings' Day or Theophany, is one of the oldest and most significant celebrations in the Christian calendar. This feast day commemorates the revelation of God incarnate in the person of Jesus Christ. The Western Church primarily celebrates the visit of the Magi, or Wise Men, to the Christ child, marking Jesus' manifestation to the Gentiles on this day. In the Eastern Church, the focus is more on the baptism of Jesus in the Jordan River, which also signifies the revelation of the Holy Trinity to the world.

The word "epiphany" itself means "manifestation" or "revelation," and this day is filled with the theme of divine revelation. It is a day of light, symbolizing how Christ is revealed to be the Light of the World, not just to the Jews but to all nations. This feast traditionally brings to a close the Christmas season, with the celebration of Christ's manifestation continuing to reverberate throughout the rest of the liturgical year.

The Gospel of Matthew tells us that the Wise Men, also called Magi, followed a star from the East to Bethlehem, where they found the Christ child and offered Him gifts of gold, frankincense, and myrrh. These gifts were prophetic: gold symbolizing his kingship, frankincense his divinity, and myrrh his future suffering and death. The journey of the Magi is symbolic of the spiritual journey that all believers are invited to undertake—a journey toward Christ, who is the ultimate revelation of God's love and salvation.

The significance of the Epiphany is profound. It represents the universal call to all people to come and worship Christ, who is the light to all nations. It is a day that invites reflection on how Christ has been revealed in our lives and how we are called to reveal Him to others. Although Epiphany is not widely celebrated in some parts of the world, in many countries, it is marked by grand celebrations, including processions, feasts, and the giving of gifts, especially in cultures where this day is the traditional time for exchanging presents rather than on Christmas Day.

Ways to Celebrate

If your children haven't already, have them check their shoes for the goodies placed in them the night before.

Do the devotion for the day.

Drink hot chocolate and eat more of the desserts you made the night before!

Gather whatever is left of your Christmas log. Traditionally, whatever is left of the Christmas Log or Yule Log is saved to light the fire of the next log the following Christmas Eve.

THE SEASON OF EPIPHANY OR EPIPHANYTIDE

The Season of Epiphany begins on January 6th, following the celebration of Christ's birth, and extends until the beginning of Lent. This season is a time of reflection on the revelation of Jesus Christ as the Light of the World, not only to the Jews but to all nations. Epiphany emphasizes the manifestation of God's presence through Christ, as seen in key events like the visit of the Magi, Jesus' baptism, and His first miracle at the wedding in Cana. Throughout this season, we are invited to meditate on how Christ is revealed to us and how we can reveal His love and truth to others.

CHRISTMAS DEVOTIONS

DECEMBER 24, CHRISTMAS EVE

Start the devotion with the lights lowered or off. The patriarch, prophet, Mary, and John the Baptist candles should already be lit.

Leader: Light and peace, in Jesus Christ our Lord.
People: **Thanks be to God.**
Leader: Let us pray.

Leader:

Lord Jesus Christ, on this day we celebrate your birth at Bethlehem and we are drawn to kneel in wonder at heaven touching earth: accept our heartfelt praise as we worship you, our Savior and our eternal God. **Amen.**

If you are using the Great Advent Candle, light it at this time. If you are using an Advent Wreath, the Jesus Candle (the white candle in the middle) is lit at this time.

All together

O gracious light, pure brightness of the everliving Father in heaven, O Jesus Christ, holy and blessed! Now, as we come to the setting of the sun, and our eyes behold the vesper light, we sing your praises, O God: Father, Son, and Holy Spirit.
You are worthy at all times to be praised by happy voices, O Son of God, O Giver of Life, and to be glorified through all the worlds.

A READING FROM HOLY SCRIPTURE

Read: Luke·2:1-20 (ESV)

1 In those days a decree went out from Caesar Augustus that all the world should be registered. 2 This was the first registration when Quirinius was governor of Syria. 3 And all went to be registered, each to his own town. 4 And Joseph also went up from Galilee, from the town of Nazareth, to Judea, to the city of David, which is called Bethlehem, because he was of the house and lineage of David, 5 to be registered with Mary, his betrothed, who was with child. 6 And while they were there, the time came for her to give birth. 7 And she gave birth to

her firstborn son and wrapped him in swaddling cloths and laid him in a manger, because there was no place for them in the inn.

8 And in the same region there were shepherds out in the field, keeping watch over their flock by night. **9** And an angel of the Lord appeared to them, and the glory of the Lord shone around them, and they were filled with great fear. **10** And the angel said to them, "Fear not, for behold, I bring you good news of great joy that will be for all the people. **11** For unto you is born this day in the city of David a Savior, who is Christ the Lord. **12** And this will be a sign for you: you will find a baby wrapped in swaddling cloths and lying in a manger." **13** And suddenly there was with the angel a multitude of the heavenly host praising God and saying, **14** "Glory to God in the highest, and on earth peace among those with whom he is pleased!"

15 When the angels went away from them into heaven, the shepherds said to one another, "Let us go over to Bethlehem and see this thing that has happened, which the Lord has made known to us." **16** And they went with haste and found Mary and Joseph, and the baby lying in a manger. **17** And when they saw it, they made known the saying that had been told them concerning this child. **18** And all who heard it wondered at what the shepherds told them. **19** But Mary treasured up all these things, pondering them in her heart. **20** And the shepherds returned, glorifying and praising God for all they had heard and seen, as it had been told them.

Use this time for other Advent observances, such as adding the final pieces of hay to the Christmas Crib, hanging the last Jesse Tree ornament, or adding baby Jesus to the Nativity Scene.

THE LORD'S PRAYER

All together
Our Father, who art in heaven,
hallowed be thy Name,
thy kingdom come, thy will be done,
on earth as it is in heaven.
Give us this day our daily bread.
And forgive us our trespasses,
as we forgive those who trespass against us.
And lead us not into temptation,
but deliver us from evil.
For thine is the kingdom,
and the power, and the glory,
for ever and ever. Amen.

THE BLESSING

Parents, lay hands on each of your children and pray this blessing over them:

The Lord bless you and keep you. **Amen.**
The Lord make his face to shine upon you and be gracious to you. **Amen.**
The Lord lift up his countenance upon you and give you peace. **Amen.**

People: **Thanks be to God.**

DECEMBER 25, CHRISTMAS DAY

Start the devotion with the lights lowered or off. All of the Advent candles and the Christ candle should already be lit.

Leader: Light and peace, in Jesus Christ our Lord.
People: **Thanks be to God.**
Leader: Let us pray.

Leader:

O God, you make us glad by the yearly festival of the birth of your only Son, Jesus Christ: Grant that we, who joyfully receive him as our Redeemer, may with sure confidence behold him when he comes to be our Judge; who lives and reigns with you and the Holy Spirit, one God, now and forever. **Amen.**

All together
O gracious light, pure brightness of the everliving Father in heaven, O Jesus Christ, holy and blessed! Now, as we come to the setting of the sun, and our eyes behold the vesper light, we sing your praises, O God: Father, Son, and Holy Spirit.
You are worthy at all times to be praised by happy voices, O Son of God, O Giver of Life, and to be glorified through all the worlds.

A READING FROM HOLY SCRIPTURE

Read: John 1:1-14 (ESV)

---

1 In the beginning was the Word, and the Word was with God, and the Word was God. **2** He was in the beginning with God. **3** All things were made through him, and without him was not any thing made that was made. **4** In him was life, and the life was the light of men. **5** The light shines in the darkness, and the darkness has not overcome it.

6 There was a man sent from God, whose name was John. **7** He came as a witness, to bear witness about the light, that all might believe through him. **8** He was not the light, but came to bear witness about the light.

9 The true light, which gives light to everyone, was coming into the world. **10** He was in the world, and the world was made through him, yet the world did not know him. **11** He came to his own, and his own people did not receive him. **12** But to all who did receive him, who believed in his name, he gave the right to become children of God, **13** who were born, not of blood nor of the will of the flesh nor of the will of man, but of God.

14 And the Word became flesh and dwelt among us, and we have seen his glory, glory as of the only Son from the Father, full of grace and truth.

Use this time for other Christmas observances: slowly move the Wise Men figures to the Nativity Scene.

THE LORD'S PRAYER

All together
Our Father, who art in heaven,
hallowed be thy Name,
thy kingdom come, thy will be done,
on earth as it is in heaven.
Give us this day our daily bread.
And forgive us our trespasses,
as we forgive those who trespass against us.
And lead us not into temptation,
but deliver us from evil.
For thine is the kingdom,
and the power, and the glory,
for ever and ever. Amen.

THE BLESSING

Parents, lay hands on each of your children and pray this blessing over them:

The Lord bless you and keep you. **Amen.**
The Lord make his face to shine upon you and be gracious to you. **Amen.**

The Lord lift up his countenance upon you and give you peace. **Amen.**

People: **Thanks be to God.**

DECEMBER 26, THE FEAST OF ST. STEPHEN

Start the devotion with the lights lowered or off. All of the Advent candles and Christ candle should already be lit.

Leader: Light and peace, in Jesus Christ our Lord.
People: **Thanks be to God.**
Leader: Let us pray.

Leader:

We give you thanks, O Lord of glory, for the example of the first martyr Stephen, who looked up to heaven and prayed for his persecutors to your Son Jesus Christ, who stands at your right hand; where he lives and reigns with you and the Holy Spirit, one God, in glory everlasting. **Amen.**

All together

O gracious light, pure brightness of the everliving Father in heaven, O Jesus Christ, holy and blessed! Now as we come to the setting of the sun, and our eyes behold the vesper light, we sing your praises, O God: Father, Son, and Holy Spirit.
You are worthy at all times to be praised by happy voices, O Son of God, O Giver of Life, and to be glorified through all the worlds.

A READING FROM HOLY SCRIPTURE

Read: Acts 6:8-15, 7:54-60

---

8 Stephen, a man full of God's grace and power, performed amazing miracles and signs among the people. **9** But one day some men from the Synagogue of Freed Slaves, as it was called, started to debate with him. They were Jews from Cyrene, Alexandria, Cilicia, and the province of Asia. **10** None of them could stand against the wisdom and the Spirit with which Stephen spoke. **11** So they persuaded some men to lie about Stephen, saying, "We heard him blaspheme Moses, and even God." **12** This roused the people, the elders, and the teachers of religious law. So they arrested Stephen and brought him before the high council. **13** The lying witnesses said, "This man is always speaking against the holy Temple and against the law of Moses. **14** We have heard him say that this Jesus of Nazareth will destroy the Temple and change the customs Moses handed down to us." **15** At this point everyone in the high council stared at Stephen, because his face became as bright as an angel's.

54 The Jewish leaders were infuriated by Stephen's accusation, and they shook their fists at him in rage. **55** But Stephen, full of the Holy Spirit, gazed steadily into heaven and saw the glory of God, and he saw Jesus standing in the place of honor at God's right hand. **56** And he told them, "Look, I see the heavens opened and the Son of Man standing in the place of honor at God's right hand!" **57** Then they put their hands over their ears and began shouting. They rushed at him **58** and dragged him out of the city and began to stone him. His accusers took off their coats and laid them at the feet of a young man named Saul. **59** As they stoned him, Stephen prayed, "Lord Jesus, receive my spirit." **60** He fell to his knees, shouting, "Lord, don't charge them with this sin!" And with that, he died.

Use this time for other Christmas observances: slowly move the Wise Men figures to the Nativity Scene.

THE LORD'S PRAYER

All together

Our Father, who art in heaven,
hallowed be thy Name,
thy kingdom come, thy will be done,
on earth as it is in heaven.
Give us this day our daily bread.
And forgive us our trespasses,
as we forgive those who trespass against us.
And lead us not into temptation,
but deliver us from evil.
For thine is the kingdom,
and the power, and the glory,
for ever and ever. Amen.

THE BLESSING

Parents, lay hands on each of your children and pray this blessing over them:

The Lord bless you and keep you. **Amen.**
The Lord make his face to shine upon you and be gracious to you. **Amen.**
The Lord lift up his countenance upon you and give you peace. **Amen.**

People: **Thanks be to God.**

DECEMBER 27, THE FEAST OF ST. JOHN

Start the devotion with the lights lowered or off. All of the Advent candles and Christ candle should already be lit.

Leader: Light and peace, in Jesus Christ our Lord.
People: **Thanks be to God.**
Leader: Let us pray.

Leader:

Shed upon your Church, O Lord, the brightness of your light, that we, being illumined by the teaching of your apostle and evangelist John, may so walk in the light of your truth, that at length we may attain to the fullness of eternal life; through Jesus Christ our Lord, who lives and reigns with you and the Holy Spirit, one God, for ever and ever. **Amen.**

All together
O gracious light, pure brightness of the everliving
Father in heaven, O Jesus Christ, holy and blessed!
Now as we come to the setting of the sun, and our eyes
behold the vesper light, we sing your praises, O God:
Father, Son, and Holy Spirit.
You are worthy at all times to be praised by happy
voices, O Son of God, O Giver of Life,
and to be glorified through all the worlds.

A READING FROM HOLY SCRIPTURE

Read: I John 1:1-9

---

1 We proclaim to you the one who existed from the beginning, whom we have heard and seen. We saw him with our own eyes and touched him with our own hands. He is the Word of life. **2** This one who is life itself was revealed to us, and we have seen him. And now we testify and proclaim to you that he is the one who is eternal life. He was with the Father, and then he was revealed to us. **3** We proclaim to you what we ourselves have actually seen and heard so that you may have fellowship with us. And our fellowship is with the Father and with his Son, Jesus Christ. **4** We are writing these things so that you may fully share our joy.

5 This is the message we heard from Jesus and now declare to you: God is light, and there is no darkness in him at all. **6** So we are lying if we say we have fellowship with God but go on living in spiritual darkness; we are not practicing the truth. **7** But if we are living in the light, as God is in the light, then we have fellowship with each other, and the blood of Jesus, his Son, cleanses us from all sin.

8 If we claim we have no sin, we are only fooling ourselves and not living in the truth. **9** But if we confess our sins to him, he is faithful and just to

forgive us our sins and to cleanse us from all
wickedness.

---

*Use this time for other Christmas observances: slowly move the
Wise Men figures to the Nativity Scene.*

THE LORD'S PRAYER

All together
**Our Father, who art in heaven,
hallowed be thy Name,
thy kingdom come, thy will be done,
on earth as it is in heaven.
Give us this day our daily bread.
And forgive us our trespasses,
as we forgive those who trespass against us.
And lead us not into temptation,
but deliver us from evil.
For thine is the kingdom,
and the power, and the glory,
for ever and ever. Amen.**

THE BLESSING

*Parents, lay hands on each of your children and pray this
blessing over them:*

The Lord bless you and keep you. **Amen.**

The Lord make his face to shine upon you and be gracious to you. **Amen.**

The Lord lift up his countenance upon you and give you peace. **Amen.**

People: **Thanks be to God.**

DECEMBER 28, THE FEAST OF THE HOLY INNOCENTS

Start the devotion with the lights lowered or off. All of the Advent candles and Christ candle should already be lit.

Leader: Light and peace, in Jesus Christ our Lord.
People: **Thanks be to God.**
Leader: Let us pray.

Leader:

We remember today, O God, the slaughter of the holy innocents of Bethlehem by King Herod. Receive, we pray, into the arms of your mercy all innocent victims; and by your great might frustrate the designs of evil tyrants and establish your rule of justice, love, and peace; through Jesus Christ our Lord, who lives and reigns with you, in the unity of the Holy Spirit, one God, forever and ever. **Amen.**

All together

**O gracious light, pure brightness of the everliving
Father in heaven, O Jesus Christ, holy and blessed!
Now as we come to the setting of the sun, and our eyes
behold the vesper light, we sing your praises, O God:
Father, Son, and Holy Spirit.
You are worthy at all times to be praised by happy
voices, O Son of God, O Giver of Life,
and to be glorified through all the worlds.**

A READING FROM HOLY SCRIPTURE

Read: Matthew 2:13-18

---

3 After the wise men were gone, an angel of the Lord appeared to Joseph in a dream. "Get up! Flee to Egypt with the child and his mother," the angel said. "Stay there until I tell you to return, because Herod is going to search for the child to kill him."

14 That night Joseph left for Egypt with the child and Mary, his mother, **15** and they stayed there until Herod's death. This fulfilled what the Lord had spoken through the prophet: "I called my Son out of Egypt."

16 Herod was furious when he realized that the wise men had outwitted him. He sent soldiers to kill all the boys in and around Bethlehem who were two years old and under, based on the wise men's report of the star's first appearance. 17 Herod's brutal action fulfilled what God had spoken through the prophet Jeremiah:

18 "A cry was heard in Ramah, weeping and great mourning. Rachel weeps for her children, refusing to be comforted, for they are dead."

Use this time for other Christmas observances: slowly move the Wise Men figures to the Nativity Scene.

THE LORD'S PRAYER

All together
**Our Father, who art in heaven,
hallowed be thy Name,
thy kingdom come, thy will be done,
on earth as it is in heaven.
Give us this day our daily bread.
And forgive us our trespasses,
as we forgive those who trespass against us.
And lead us not into temptation,
but deliver us from evil.
For thine is the kingdom,
and the power, and the glory,
for ever and ever. Amen.**

THE BLESSING

Parents, lay hands on each of your children and pray this blessing over them:

The Lord bless you and keep you. **Amen.**
The Lord make his face to shine upon you and be gracious to you. **Amen.**
The Lord lift up his countenance upon you and give you peace. **Amen.**

People: **Thanks be to God.**

DECEMBER 29

Start the devotion with the lights lowered or off. All of the Advent candles and Christ candle should already be lit.

Leader: Light and peace, in Jesus Christ our Lord.
People: **Thanks be to God.**
Leader: Let us pray.

Leader:

Almighty God, you have poured upon us the new light of your incarnate Word: Grant that this light, enkindled in our hearts, may shine forth in our lives; through Jesus Christ our Lord, who lives and reigns with you, in the unity of the Holy Spirit, one God, now and for ever. **Amen.**

All together

O gracious light, pure brightness of the everliving Father in heaven, O Jesus Christ, holy and blessed! Now as we come to the setting of the sun, and our eyes behold the vesper light, we sing your praises, O God: Father, Son, and Holy Spirit.
You are worthy at all times to be praised by happy voices, O Son of God, O Giver of Life,
and to be glorified through all the worlds.

A READING FROM HOLY SCRIPTURE

Read: Galatians 3:23-25; 4:4-7

---

23 Before the way of faith in Christ was available to us, we were placed under guard by the law. We were kept in protective custody, so to speak, until the way of faith was revealed.

24 Let me put it another way. The law was our guardian until Christ came; it protected us until we could be made right with God through faith. **25** And now that the way of faith has come, we no longer need the law as our guardian.

4 But when the right time came, God sent his Son, born of a woman, subject to the law. **5** God sent him to buy freedom for us who were slaves to the law, so that he could adopt us as his very own children. **6** And because we are his children, God has sent the Spirit of his Son into our hearts, prompting us to call out, "Abba, Father." 7 Now you are no longer a slave but God's own child. And since you are his child, God has made you his heir.

Use this time for other Christmas observances: slowly move the Wise Men figures to the Nativity Scene.

THE LORD'S PRAYER

All together
Our Father, who art in heaven,
hallowed be thy Name,
thy kingdom come, thy will be done,
on earth as it is in heaven.
Give us this day our daily bread.
And forgive us our trespasses,
as we forgive those who trespass against us.
And lead us not into temptation,
but deliver us from evil.
For thine is the kingdom,
and the power, and the glory,
for ever and ever. Amen.

THE BLESSING

Parents, lay hands on each of your children and pray this blessing over them:

The Lord bless you and keep you. **Amen.**
The Lord make his face to shine upon you and be gracious to you. **Amen.**
The Lord lift up his countenance upon you and give you peace. **Amen.**

People: **Thanks be to God.**

DECEMBER 30

Start the devotion with the lights lowered or off. All of the Advent candles and Christ candle should already be lit.

Leader: Light and peace, in Jesus Christ our Lord.
People: **Thanks be to God.**
Leader: Let us pray.

Leader:

Almighty God, you have given your only-begotten Son tovtake our nature upon him, and to be born his day of a pure virgin: Grant that we, who have been born again and made your children by adoption and grace, may daily be renewed by your Holy Spirit; through our Lord Jesus Christ, to whom with you and the same Spirit be honor and glory, now and for ever. **Amen.**

All together

O gracious light, pure brightness of the everliving
Father in heaven, O Jesus Christ, holy and blessed!
Now as we come to the setting of the sun, and our eyes
behold the vesper light, we sing your praises, O God:
Father, Son, and Holy Spirit.
You are worthy at all times to be praised by happy
voices, O Son of God, O Giver of Life,
and to be glorified through all the worlds.

A READING FROM HOLY SCRIPTURE

Read: Ephesians 1:5-6

---

5 God decided in advance to adopt us into his own family by bringing us to himself through Jesus Christ. This is what he wanted to do, and it gave him great pleasure. **6** So we praise God for the glorious grace he has poured out on us who belong to his dear Son.

Use this time for other Christmas observances: slowly move the Wise Men figures to the Nativity Scene.

THE LORD'S PRAYER

All together

Our Father, who art in heaven,
hallowed be thy Name,
thy kingdom come, thy will be done,
on earth as it is in heaven.
Give us this day our daily bread.
And forgive us our trespasses,
as we forgive those who trespass against us.
And lead us not into temptation,
but deliver us from evil.
For thine is the kingdom,
and the power, and the glory,
for ever and ever. Amen.

THE BLESSING

Parents, lay hands on each of your children and pray this blessing over them:

The Lord bless you and keep you. **Amen.**
The Lord make his face to shine upon you and be gracious to you. **Amen.**
The Lord lift up his countenance upon you and give you peace. **Amen.**

People: **Thanks be to God.**

DECEMBER 31 (NEW YEAR'S EVE)

Start the devotion with the lights lowered or off. All of the Advent candles and Christ candle should already be lit.

Leader: Light and peace, in Jesus Christ our Lord.
People: **Thanks be to God.**
Leader: Let us pray.

Leader:

Almighty God, you are the source of all life, you are the giver of all blessings, and the Savior of all who turn to you: Have mercy upon this nation; deliver us from lies, anger, and disobedience; turn our feet into your paths; and grant that we may serve you in peace; through Jesus Christ our Lord. **Amen.**

All together
O gracious light, pure brightness of the everliving
Father in heaven, O Jesus Christ, holy and blessed!
Now as we come to the setting of the sun, and our eyes
behold the vesper light, we sing your praises, O God:
Father, Son, and Holy Spirit.
You are worthy at all times to be praised by happy
voices, O Son of God, O Giver of Life,
and to be glorified through all the worlds.

A READING FROM HOLY SCRIPTURE

Read: Ecclesiastes 3:1-15

---

3 For everything there is a season, and a time for every matter under heaven: 2 a time to be born, and a time to die; a time to plant, and a time to pluck up what is planted; 3 a time to kill, and a time to heal; a time to break down, and a time to build up; 4 a time to weep, and a time to laugh; a time to mourn, and a time to dance; 5 a time to cast away stones, and a time to gather stones together; a time to embrace, and a time to refrain from embracing; 6 a time to seek, and a time to lose; a time to keep, and a time to cast away; 7 a time to tear, and a time to sew; a time to keep silence, and a time to speak; 8 a time to love, and a time to hate; a time for war, and a time for peace.

9 What gain has the worker from his toil? 10 I have seen the business that God has given to the children of man to be busy with. 11 He has made everything beautiful in its time. Also, he has put eternity into man's heart, yet so that he cannot find out what God has done from the beginning to the end. 12 I perceived that there is nothing better for them than to be joyful and to do good as long as they live; 13 also that everyone should eat and drink and take pleasure in all his toil—this is God's gift to man.

14 I perceived that whatever God does endures forever; nothing can be added to it, nor anything taken from it. God has done it, so that people fear before him. **15** That which is, already has been; that which is to be, already has been; and God seeks what has been driven away.

Use this time for other Christmas observances: slowly move the Wise Men figures to the Nativity Scene.

THE LORD'S PRAYER

All together
Our Father, who art in heaven,
hallowed be thy Name,
thy kingdom come, thy will be done,
on earth as it is in heaven.
Give us this day our daily bread.
And forgive us our trespasses,
as we forgive those who trespass against us.
And lead us not into temptation,
but deliver us from evil.
For thine is the kingdom,
and the power, and the glory,
for ever and ever. Amen.

THE BLESSING

Parents, lay hands on each of your children and pray this blessing over them:

The Lord bless you and keep you. **Amen.**
The Lord make his face to shine upon you and be gracious to you. **Amen.**
The Lord lift up his countenance upon you and give you peace. **Amen.**

People: **Thanks be to God.**

JANUARY 1, THE FEAST OF THE HOLY NAME

Start the devotion with the lights lowered or off. All of the Advent candles and Christ candle should already be lit.

Leader: Light and peace, in Jesus Christ our Lord.
People: **Thanks be to God.**
Leader: Let us pray.

Leader:

Eternal Father, you gave to your incarnate Son the holy name of Jesus to be the sign of our salvation: Plant in every heart, we pray, the love of him who is the Savior of the world, our Lord Jesus Christ; who lives and reigns with you and the Holy Spirit, one God, in glory everlasting. **Amen.**

All together

**O gracious light, pure brightness of the everliving
Father in heaven, O Jesus Christ, holy and blessed!
Now as we come to the setting of the sun, and our eyes
behold the vesper light, we sing your praises, O God:
Father, Son, and Holy Spirit.
You are worthy at all times to be praised by happy
voices, O Son of God, O Giver of Life,
and to be glorified through all the worlds.**

A READING FROM HOLY SCRIPTURE

Read: Philippians 2:5-11

---

5 You must have the same attitude that Christ Jesus
had. **6** Though he was God, he did not think of
equality with God as something to cling to.
7 Instead, he gave up his divine privileges; he took
the humble position of a slave and was born as a
human being. When he appeared in human form,
8 he humbled himself in obedience to God and died
a criminal's death on a cross. **9** Therefore, God
elevated him to the place of highest honor and gave
him the name above all other names, **10** that at the
name of Jesus, every knee should bow, in heaven and
on earth and under the earth, **11** and every tongue
declare that Jesus Christ is Lord, to the glory of God
the Father.

Use this time for other Christmas observances: slowly move the Wise Men figures to the Nativity Scene.

THE LORD'S PRAYER

All together
Our Father, who art in heaven,
hallowed be thy Name,
thy kingdom come, thy will be done,
on earth as it is in heaven.
Give us this day our daily bread.
And forgive us our trespasses,
as we forgive those who trespass against us.
And lead us not into temptation,
but deliver us from evil.
For thine is the kingdom,
and the power, and the glory,
for ever and ever. Amen.

THE BLESSING

Parents, lay hands on each of your children and pray this blessing over them:

The Lord bless you and keep you. **Amen.**
The Lord make his face to shine upon you and be gracious to you. **Amen.**
The Lord lift up his countenance upon you and give you peace. **Amen.**

People: **Thanks be to God.**

JANUARY 2

Start the devotion with the lights lowered or off. All of the Advent candles and Christ candle should already be lit.

Leader: Light and peace, in Jesus Christ our Lord.
People: **Thanks be to God.**
Leader: Let us pray.

Leader:

O God, who wonderfully created, and yet more wonderfully restored, the dignity of human nature: Grant that we may share the divine life of him who humbled his life to share our humanity, your Son Jesus Christ our Lord; who lives and reigns with you, in the unity of the Holy Spirit, one God, for ever and ever. **Amen.**

All together
O gracious light, pure brightness of the everliving Father in heaven, O Jesus Christ, holy and blessed! Now as we come to the setting of the sun, and our eyes behold the vesper light, we sing your praises, O God: Father, Son, and Holy Spirit. You are worthy at all times to be praised by happy voices, O Son of God, O Giver of Life, and to be glorified through all the worlds.

A READING FROM HOLY SCRIPTURE

Read: Hebrews 2:14-17

---

14 Because God's children are human beings, made of flesh and blood, the Son also became flesh and blood. For only as a human being could he die, and only by dying could he break the power of the devil, who had the power of death. **15** Only in this way could he set free all who have lived their lives as slaves to the fear of dying.

16 We also know that the Son did not come to help angels; he came to help the descendants of Abraham. **17** Therefore, it was necessary for him to be made in every respect like us, his brothers and sisters, so that he could be our merciful and faithful High Priest before God. Then he could offer a sacrifice that would take away the sins of the people.

Use this time for other Christmas observances: slowly move the Wise Men figures to the Nativity Scene.

THE LORD'S PRAYER

All together
Our Father, who art in heaven,
hallowed be thy Name,
thy kingdom come, thy will be done,

on earth as it is in heaven.
Give us this day our daily bread.
And forgive us our trespasses,
as we forgive those who trespass against us.
And lead us not into temptation,
but deliver us from evil.
For thine is the kingdom,
and the power, and the glory,
for ever and ever. Amen.

THE BLESSING

Parents, lay hands on each of your children and pray this blessing over them:

The Lord bless you and keep you. **Amen.**
The Lord make his face to shine upon you and be gracious to you. **Amen.**
The Lord lift up his countenance upon you and give you peace. **Amen.**

People: **Thanks be to God.**

JANUARY 3

Start the devotion with the lights lowered or off. All of the Advent candles and Christ candle should already be lit.

Leader: Light and peace, in Jesus Christ our Lord.
People: **Thanks be to God.**

Leader: Let us pray.

Leader:

Lord Jesus Christ, your birth at Bethlehem draws us to kneel in wonder at heaven touching earth: accept our heartfelt praise as we worship you, our Saviour and our eternal God. **Amen.**

All together
O gracious light, pure brightness of the everliving Father in heaven, O Jesus Christ, holy and blessed! Now as we come to the setting of the sun, and our eyes behold the vesper light, we sing your praises, O God: Father, Son, and Holy Spirit. You are worthy at all times to be praised by happy voices, O Son of God, O Giver of Life, and to be glorified through all the worlds.

A READING FROM HOLY SCRIPTURE

Read: Isaiah 9:6

---

9 For a child is born to us, a son is given to us. The government will rest on his shoulders. And he will be called: Wonderful Counselor, Mighty God, Everlasting Father, Prince of Peace.

Use this time for other Christmas observances: slowly move the Wise Men figures to the Nativity Scene.

THE LORD'S PRAYER

All together
**Our Father, who art in heaven,
hallowed be thy Name,
thy kingdom come, thy will be done,
on earth as it is in heaven.
Give us this day our daily bread.
And forgive us our trespasses,
as we forgive those who trespass against us.
And lead us not into temptation,
but deliver us from evil.
For thine is the kingdom,
and the power, and the glory,
for ever and ever. Amen.**

THE BLESSING

Parents, lay hands on each of your children and pray this blessing over them:

The Lord bless you and keep you. **Amen.**
The Lord make his face to shine upon you and be gracious to you. **Amen.**
The Lord lift up his countenance upon you and give you peace. **Amen.**

People: **Thanks be to God.**

JANUARY 4

Start the devotion with the lights lowered or off. All of the Advent candles and Christ candle should already be lit.

Leader: Light and peace, in Jesus Christ our Lord.
People: **Thanks be to God.**
Leader: Let us pray.

Leader:

God our Father, in love you sent your Son that the world may have life: lead us to seek him among the outcast and to find him in those in need, for Jesus Christ's sake. **Amen.**

All together
O gracious light, pure brightness of the everliving Father in heaven, O Jesus Christ, holy and blessed! Now as we come to the setting of the sun, and our eyes behold the vesper light, we sing your praises, O God: Father, Son, and Holy Spirit.
You are worthy at all times to be praised by happy voices, O Son of God, O Giver of Life,
and to be glorified through all the worlds.

A READING FROM HOLY SCRIPTURE

Read: Matthew 25:34-40

---

34 "Then the King will say to those on his right, 'Come, you who are blessed by my Father, inherit the Kingdom prepared for you from the creation of the world. **35** For I was hungry, and you fed me. I was thirsty, and you gave me a drink. I was a stranger, and you invited me into your home. **36** I was naked, and you gave me clothing. I was sick, and you cared for me. I was in prison, and you visited me.'

37 "Then these righteous ones will reply, 'Lord, when did we ever see you hungry and feed you? Or thirsty and give you something to drink? **38** Or a stranger and show you hospitality? Or naked and give you clothing? **39** When did we ever see you sick or in prison and visit you?'

40 "And the King will say, 'I tell you the truth, when you did it to one of the least of these my brothers and sisters, you were doing it to me!'

Use this time for other Christmas observances: slowly move the Wise Men figures to the Nativity Scene.

THE LORD'S PRAYER

All together
Our Father, who art in heaven,
hallowed be thy Name,
thy kingdom come, thy will be done,
on earth as it is in heaven.
Give us this day our daily bread.
And forgive us our trespasses,
as we forgive those who trespass against us.
And lead us not into temptation,
but deliver us from evil.
For thine is the kingdom,
and the power, and the glory,
for ever and ever. Amen.

THE BLESSING

Parents, lay hands on each of your children and pray this blessing over them:

The Lord bless you and keep you. **Amen.**
The Lord make his face to shine upon you and be gracious to you. **Amen.**
The Lord lift up his countenance upon you and give you peace. **Amen.**

People: **Thanks be to God.**

JANUARY 5

Start the devotion with the lights lowered or off. All of the Advent candles and Christ candle should already be lit.

Leader: Light and peace, in Jesus Christ our Lord.
People: **Thanks be to God.**
Leader: Let us pray.

Leader:

O God, by the leading of the star you manifested your only Son to the peoples of the earth: Lead us, who know you now by faith, to your presence, where we may see your glory face to face; through Jesus Christ our Lord, who lives and reigns with you and the Holy Spirit, one God, now and forever. **Amen.**

All together
O gracious light, pure brightness of the everliving
Father in heaven, O Jesus Christ, holy and blessed!
Now as we come to the setting of the sun, and our eyes
behold the vesper light, we sing your praises, O God:
Father, Son, and Holy Spirit.
You are worthy at all times to be praised by happy
voices, O Son of God, O Giver of Life,
and to be glorified through all the worlds.

A READING FROM HOLY SCRIPTURE

Read: Matthew 2:1-12

---

2 Jesus was born in Bethlehem in Judea, during the reign of King Herod. About that time some wise men from eastern lands arrived in Jerusalem, asking, **2** "Where is the newborn king of the Jews? We saw his star as it rose, and we have come to worship him."

3 King Herod was deeply disturbed when he heard this, as was everyone in Jerusalem. **4** He called a meeting of the leading priests and teachers of religious law and asked, "Where is the Messiah supposed to be born?"

5 "In Bethlehem in Judea," they said, "for this is what the prophet wrote:

6 'And you, O Bethlehem in the land of Judah, are not least among the ruling cities of Judah, for a ruler will come from you who will be the shepherd for my people Israel.'"

7 Then Herod called for a private meeting with the wise men, and he learned from them the time when the star first appeared. **8** Then he told them, "Go to Bethlehem and search carefully for the child. And when you find him, come back and tell me so that I can go and worship him, too!"

9 After this interview the wise men went their way. And the star they had seen in the east guided them to Bethlehem. It went ahead of them and stopped over the place where the child was. **10** When they saw the star, they were filled with joy! **11** They entered the house and saw the child with his mother, Mary, and they bowed down and worshiped him. Then they opened their treasure chests and gave him gifts of gold, frankincense, and myrrh.

12 When it was time to leave, they returned to their own country by another route, for God had warned them in a dream not to return to Herod.

Use this time for other Christmas observances: slowly move the Wise Men figures to the Nativity Scene.

THE LORD'S PRAYER

All together
Our Father, who art in heaven,
hallowed be thy Name,
thy kingdom come, thy will be done,
on earth as it is in heaven.
Give us this day our daily bread.
And forgive us our trespasses,
as we forgive those who trespass against us.
And lead us not into temptation,
but deliver us from evil.

**For thine is the kingdom,
and the power, and the glory,
for ever and ever. Amen.**

THE BLESSING

Parents, lay hands on each of your children and pray this blessing over them:

The Lord bless you and keep you. **Amen.**
The Lord make his face to shine upon you and be gracious to you. **Amen.**
The Lord lift up his countenance upon you and give you peace. **Amen.**

People: **Thanks be to God.**

CHRISTMASTIDE RECIPES

*T*raditional Christmas recipes from around the world.

BUBBLE AND SQUEAK

Made on the Feast of St. Stephen.

> 1 pound brussels sprouts, washed and
>   halved lengthwise
> 1 pound carrots, peeled and coarsely
>   chopped
> 2 tablespoons olive oil, divided
> 4 pounds potatoes, peeled and cut
>   into large chunks
> 8 tablespoons butter, divided
> 1 teaspoon white pepper plus more to
>   taste

1 teaspoon salt plus more to taste

1 onion, coarsely chopped

Preheat the oven to 400 degrees. In a roasting pan, add the Brussels sprouts and carrots, then drizzle with 1 tablespoon of olive oil. Roast until dark and caramelized, about 50 minutes, then set aside.

As the vegetables roast, boil the potatoes. Add them to a pot and fill it with enough water to cover it by 1 inch; boil until tender, about 15 minutes. Strain and mash with 4 tablespoons of butter, white pepper, and salt; set aside.

Warm a skillet or pan over medium heat, then add the remaining olive oil and butter and warm for 1 minute. Add the onion and sauté until softened, about 4 minutes, then add the potatoes and winter vegetables. Mash the vegetables together, then gently pat them into a thick pancake. Pan-fry until browned on the bottom, about 25 minutes, then flip and mash together. Pat flat and pan-fry again until brown and crispy, another 25 minutes, then mash once more. Season with salt and pepper to taste and serve.

Recipe from www.foodandwine.com/recipes/bubble-and-squeak

BUCHE DE NOEL OR CHRISTMAS LOG

Made on Christmas Eve or Christmas Day.

Sponge Cake:

> 4 eggs, separated and at room
>   temperature
> 1 cup sugar
> 1/4 cup hot water
> Grated rind of 1 lemon
> 1 teaspoon lemon juice
> 1/2 teaspoon vanilla
> 1 cup sifted flour
> 1 teaspoon baking powder
> 1/4 teaspoon salt
> A few tablespoons of rum (optional)
> confectioner's sugar

Preheat oven to 400 degrees. Grease a jelly-roll pan, 10 by 15 inches. Line the pan with waxed paper and grease the paper.

Beat the yolks until light and lemon colored. Gradually add the sugar, beating until very thick. Beat in the hot water, lemon rind, juice, and vanilla.

Sift the flour with the baking powder and salt, and gradually beat into the egg mixture. Whip the egg whites until stiff but not dry. Fold gently but thoroughly into the batter.

Pour it into the jelly roll pan. Bake for 12 to 15 minutes, or until the cake is lightly browned.

As soon as the cake is done, sprinkle it with the rum if you wish. Spread a clean, damp kitchen towel on the counter. Cover it with waxed paper. Sprinkle the paper with confectioner sugar. Invert the cake onto the waxed paper. Peel the paper off of the cake and trim the cake if too crusty. Roll up the cake along the long side with the towel and waxed paper. Let it cool to room temperature.

Mocha Cream Icing:

> 4 egg yolks
> 1 1/4 cups sugar
> 1/3 cup water
> 2 teaspoons vanilla extract
> 2 teaspoons instant coffee
> 2 ounces unsweetened chocolate,
>   melted and cooled
> 3 sticks of butter, at room
>   temperature

Beat the yolks until light-colored and thick. Combine the sugar and water in a saucepan. Cook to the soft-ball stage: about 234 degrees on a candy thermometer. Beating constantly, add the eggs to the syrup. Continue beating until the mixture is cool. Stir in the vanilla extract, coffee, and chocolate. Gradually beat in the butter. Cool the icing in the refrigerator if it is too soft.

Unroll the cake. Spread it with half of the icing. Without the paper and the towel, roll it up as tightly as possible without damaging it. Chill for several hours. Chill the icing as well. Trim the ends of the cake on the diagonal; reserve the scraps. Frost the cake with most of the remaining icing. Cut the scraps to resemble knot holes. Set them on the main log and ice them. Using the tines of a fork, make marks on the surface of the cake to look like bark.

Recipe from A Continual Feast

BUNUELOS (MEXICAN FRITTERS)

Made on Christmas Eve or Christmas Day.

Fritters:

3 cups flour
1 tablespoon sugar
2 teaspoons baking powder
1/2 teaspoon salt
3/4 cup milk
1 egg
2 tablespoons lard, melted and cooled
2 teaspoons vanilla
Vegetable oil, for frying

Cinnamon Sugar:

> 1 cup sugar
> 1 tablespoon cinnamon

Anise Syrup (optional):

> 2 cups water
> 8 ounces Mexican brown sugar,
>   coarsely chopped
> 1 teaspoon grated lime peel
> 1 teaspoon grated orange peel
> 2 cinnamon sticks
> 2 teaspoons anise seed

For the fritters:

Mix flour, sugar, baking powder, and salt in a medium bowl. Set aside. Mix milk, egg, lard, and vanilla in a large bowl until well blended. Gradually add the flour mixture, stirring constantly to form a slightly sticky dough. Turn the dough out onto a lightly floured surface. Incorporate additional flour, a tablespoon of flour at a time, until the dough is no longer sticky. Divide dough into 16 equal pieces. Shape each into a ball. Place in bowl. Cover with plastic wrap. Let dough rest for 30 minutes.

For the cinnamon sugar:

Mix sugar and cinnamon in a medium bowl. Set aside. For the Anise Syrup, mix water, Mexican brown sugar, lime peel, orange peel, cinnamon sticks, and anise seed in a heavy-bottomed 3-quart saucepan. Cook on medium heat for 5 minutes, stirring to dissolve Mexican brown sugar. Bring to boil on medium-high heat. Boil for 20 minutes or until syrup thinly coats a spoon. Strain and set aside at room temperature. (Anise Syrup can be made 3 to 4 days ahead. Cover and refrigerate. Rewarm before using.)

Roll each ball of dough into a 6-inch round on a lightly floured surface. Stack dough rounds between wax paper or plastic wrap. Let stand for 10 minutes.

Pour vegetable oil into a heavy large skillet or saucepan to a depth of 1 inch (about 2 cups oil). Heat oil on medium-high heat to 365°F to 370°F on a deep-fry thermometer. Fry dough rounds, 1 at a time, for 2 minutes or until golden and puffed, turning once using tongs. Drain on paper towels. Sprinkle each fritter with 1 tablespoon cinnamon sugar mixture. Serve with warm Anise Syrup, if desired.

Recipe from McCormick.com

CHICKADEE PUDDING

Served to the birds on Christmas Eve.

>   Ground suet
>   Flour
>   Sugar
>   Cornmeal
>   Old cake, bread, doughnuts
>   Wild Bird Seed
>   Peanut Butter
>   Ground apples
>   Nuts
>   Raisins
>   Bacon Fat

Mix all of the ingredients, except the bacon fat in whatever proportions you happen to have on hand. Melt plenty of fat and, while it's still hot, pour it over the mixture, stirring well. Pour the mixture into disposable aluminum pie plates. Freeze. Wrap up with a pretty ribbon.

CHRISTMAS PUNCH

Made on Christmas Eve or Christmas Day.

> 1 sliced pineapple
> 1 lb. sugar
> 1 bottle claret
> 1 bottle of red wine
> 1/2 bottle rum
> juice of 4 lemons
> juice of 4 oranges
> 1 pint water
> grated rind of 1 lemon
> grated rind of 1 orange
> 4 whole oranges cut in pieces
> 1 stick cinnamon, broken up
> 1 vanilla bean
> 1/2 cup maraschino cherries
> 1 bottle champagne

Boil spices thoroughly with the water. Remove them and pour the water into a large earthenware pot. Add lemon and orange and rind, as well as pineapple and sugar (fruit and sugar prepared in a separate dish). Then add wine and rum, cover, and heat. Add champagne before serving. (This is only for adults! See Christmas Punch for Children for a kid-friendly recipe)

Recipe from Maria Von Trapp

CHRISTMAS PUNCH FOR CHILDREN

Made on Christmas Eve or Christmas Day.

> 1 quart grape juice
> 2 quarts water
> 2 cups sugar
> 1/2 teaspoon whole cloves
> 1 stick cinnamon
> juice of 2 lemons
> juice of 2 oranges
> rind of 2 lemons
> rind of 2 oranges

Boil sugar, water, lemon rind, and spices until flavored. Mix with the rest of the ingredients, boil for five minutes, and serve hot in punch glasses.

Recipe from Maria Von Trapp

COVENTRY GOD CAKES

Made on the Feast of the Holy Name.

Rich shortcrust:

> 2 cups flour
> 1 tsp salt
> 1 Tbl. confectioner's sugar
> 8 Tbsp cold butter, cut into pieces
> 1 egg, lightly beaten

1 Tbsp milk or water

Filling:

¼ butter, room temperature

¼ cup sugar

¾ cup currants

¼ cup candied lemon peel, finely
chopped

Grated rind of ½ a lemon

¼ tsp nutmeg

½ tsp allspice

Combine the flour and salt in a mixing bowl. If you wish, stir in the sugar. Using the tips of your fingers or two knives, work in the butter until the mixture resembles a coarse meal. Make a well and add the egg and milk. Mix briefly with a fork. Form the dough into a ball. Wrap it in plastic wrap and chill it in the refrigerator for at least ½ hour.

Preheat the oven to 425 degrees Fahrenheit. Butter 2 baking sheets.

To make the filling: Cream the butter with the sugar until fluffy. Stir in the remaining ingredients, blending thoroughly.

On a lightly floured surface, roll the dough out thin. Cut into four-inch squares. Reroll the scraps. Place 1 heaping teaspoon of filling near one corner of each square, leaving

½ inch of dough uncovered. Lightly moisten the edges of the pastry. Fold from corner to corner to make triangles. Seal the edges with your fingers, then with the tines of a fork.

Place the cakes on the baking sheets and bake for 10 to 15 minutes, or until golden brown.

Recipe from A Continual Feast

EGGNOG

Made on Christmas Eve and Christmas Day.

> 4 egg yolks
> 1/3 cup sugar, plus 1 tablespoon
> 1 pint whole milk
> 1 cup heavy cream
> 3 ounces bourbon
> 1 teaspoon freshly grated nutmeg
> 4 egg whites*

In the bowl of a stand mixer, beat the egg yolks until they lighten in color. Gradually add the 1/3 cup sugar and continue to beat until it is completely dissolved. Add the milk, cream, bourbon, and nutmeg and stir to combine.

Place the egg whites in the bowl of a stand mixer and beat to soft peaks. With the mixer still running gradually add 1 tablespoon of sugar and beat until stiff peaks form. Whisk the egg whites into the mixture. Chill and serve.

Cook's Note: For cooked eggnog, follow the procedure below.

In the bowl of a stand mixer, beat the egg yolks until they lighten in color. Gradually add 1/3 cup sugar and continue to beat until it is completely dissolved. Set aside.

In a medium saucepan, over high heat, combine milk, heavy cream, and nutmeg and bring just to a boil, stirring occasionally. Remove from the heat and gradually temper the hot mixture into the egg and sugar mixture. Then return everything to the pot and cook until the mixture reaches 160 degrees F. Remove from the heat, stir in bourbon, pour into a medium mixing bowl, and set in the refrigerator to chill.

In a medium mixing bowl, beat the egg whites to soft peaks. With the mixer running gradually add 1 tablespoon of sugar and beat until stiff peaks form. Whisk the egg whites into the chilled mixture.

Recipe from foodnetwork.com

FRUITCAKE

Served throughout the season of Christmas.

> 1 lb. butter, room temperature
> 2 cups sugar
> 6 eggs
> 1/4 cup rum, brandy, sherry, whiskey
> 1 teaspoon vanilla
> 4 cups of flour
> 2 teaspoons baking powder
> 2 teaspoons salt
> 2 1/2 cups raisins (half dark and half light)
> 2 cups currants
> 1 1/2 cups mixed candies fruit peel

Glaze:

> Confectioner's Sugar
> Water or milk
> Grated lemon rind
> Whole glace cherries or pecan halves

Cream the butter with the sugar until fluffy. Stir in the eggs, one at a time, blending thoroughly after each addition. Stir in the spirits and the vanilla.

Sift the flour with the baking powder and salt. Stir the

flour into the buttered mixture until thoroughly mixed. Add the raisins, currants, and candied fruits.

You can bake the cakes in large loaf pans or a large tube pan. Butter the pans generously.

Pour the batter into the pans. Bake at 300 degrees for 2 hours, or until a toothpick inserted comes out clean. You may cover cakes with aluminum foil toward the end of the baking time if they are getting too brown on top.

Let the cake or cakes cool for 10 to 15 minutes, then remove them from the pans.

Make a thin glaze of confectioner's sugar mixed with a little water or milk, and a little grated lemon rind. Decorate the cakes with whole glace cherries and pecans, and paint with the glaze.

Recipe from A Continual Feast

KNODEL (POTATO DUMPLINGS)

Made on Christmas Day

> 2 lb starchy potatoes such as russet
>   potatoes
> 1 cup potato starch (you can also use
>   corn starch if you can't find potato
>   starch)
> 1 egg large
> 1 teaspoon salt

Peel and cut up the potatoes into smaller chunks, so they boil faster. Boil in unsalted water until soft for about 10 to 15 minutes. If you poke them with a fork or a knife, they should slide in easily when they're done.

Drain and purée with a Spätzle press, potato masher, or handheld mixer.

Fill the pot with water again, add some salt, and bring to a boil.

No-measurement method: Press the mashed potatoes down in a bowl, divide them into fourths using a knife or spatula, and shovel up ¼ of the potatoes, moving it onto the other ¾.

Then fill the empty quarter with potato starch OR measure out the starch to add, but I find the no-to to be much simpler and fast.

Add the egg and some salt and mix together with a fork until it cooled down enough to handle with your hands.

Divide dough into 10 pieces (I shape a log, then cut it up). Shape 10 balls using your palms and drop them into gently simmering water.

Simmer for about 10 minutes. Your dumplings will have floated to the top. Use a skimmer to remove the dumplings, and run some cool water over them.

Recipe from https://dirndlkitchen.com/potato-dumplings-wusthof-knife-giveaway/

KOURABIEDES (GREEK BUTTER COOKIES)

Made on Christmas Eve and Christmas Day.

> 1 1/2 cups cold unsalted butter
> 1 1/4 cups almonds, roughly chopped
>   or almond slivers, roasted
> 1/4 cup almonds (whole) or almond
>   slivers, raw
> 1/2 cup icing sugar
> 1 tbsp rose water
> 1/2 tsp vanilla extract
> 1 tbsp baking powder
> a pinch of salt
> 3 1/4 cups all-purpose flour
> lots of icing sugar for powdering

Preheat the oven to 390F. Place the roughly chopped almonds or almond silvers on a baking tray and sprinkle with some water. Bake them for 7-8 minutes, until roasted, being careful not to burn them. Set aside or put in the fridge to cool.

In a blender, add the raw almonds or the pistachios and blend, until powdered. Set aside.

In a food processor, add the cold butter and sugar; mix for about 10 seconds, until the butter 'breaks' and is completely dissolved. Add the powdered almonds, a pinch of salt, the rosewater, and the vanilla extract; mix for 10-

20 seconds, until combined. At the end, add the baking powder and flour and mix again for 10-15 seconds.

Place the mixture in a large bowl and add the roasted almonds; blend lightly with your hands. For the kourabiedes to remain fluffy, it is important that the butter doesn't warm up and melt. So wait for a while for the roasted almonds to cool, before adding them to the butter mixture.

Preheat the oven to 340F. Layer the bottom of 2 baking trays with parchment paper and form the kourabiedes.

Roll 1 tbsp of the dough into a ball, place on the baking tray, and push with your finger in the middle, to form a little dimple. Continue with the rest of the dough. Place in the fridge for 5 minutes until you prepare your next tray.

Place the baking trays with the kourabiedes in a second and fourth rack of the oven. Bake for approx. 15-20 minutes, until they have a very faint golden tint and are cooked through. Be careful not to overbake them.

Leave the kourabiedes aside to cool down for a while. If you try to lift them, while still warm, they will break!

Spray the kourabiedes with rosewater and sift with icing sugar. Enjoy!

Recipe from https://www.mygreekdish.com/recipe/kourabiedes-greek-christmas-butter-cookies/

KRAPFEN

Made on New Year's Eve.

> 3/4 cup warm milk
> 4 ½ tablespoons granulated sugar
> 1 ¾ teaspoons active dry yeast
> 3 egg yolks from large eggs
> 4 ½ tablespoons unsalted butter,
>   melted and cooled
> 1 teaspoon vanilla extract
> 2 teaspoons rum (any will do)
> 3/4 teaspoon fine salt
> 2 2/3 cups all-purpose flour plus up
>   to 2 tablespoons more if you are
>   kneading by hand
> Vegetable oil (you will need at least 2
>   cups, usually more depending on
>   the size of your pan)
> About 3/4 cup smooth, fine-textured
>   apricot jam - not chunky (stir in 1
>   teaspoon rum if you like)
> Confectioners' sugar
> Medium-sized frying pan or saucepan
>   with lid
> Piping bag with a round tip

You can either make the dough using a mixer with dough hooks attached or knead it by hand. I recommend using a mixer since the dough is pretty moist and sticky. I've included both methods.

Combine milk and sugar in a large mixing bowl. Sprinkle the yeast over the milk and set it aside for 5-10 minutes for the yeast to dissolve.

Stir in egg yolks, lukewarm butter, vanilla, rum, and salt using a hand whisk until well combined.

Add half of the flour and stir thoroughly using the hand whisk (the dough should resemble pancake batter at this point).

With a sturdy spoon (or a mixer with dough hooks) stir in the rest of the flour. Mix the ingredients until they come together into a sticky dough.

Add the rest of the flour and knead it for 5 minutes until smooth.

With floured or greased hands, try to fold the edges of the dough into the center a couple of times. If the dough is too sticky, add up to 2 more tablespoons (not more) flour, mix it into the dough, and try again. If still too sticky, cover the bowl and let the dough rest for 5 minutes. After that, the dough will be better to work with.

In the bowl, knead the dough (or fold the edges over itself) until smooth, about 5 to 10 minutes. The dough should still be moist and a little sticky.

Grease a clean mixing bowl and return the dough to the

bowl. Set in a warm place to rise until doubled in bulk, about 1 to 1 ½ hours.

Plop the dough upside down onto a floured surface, lightly flour the top, and roll the dough to 1/2 to 3/4-inch thickness.

Prepare a baking pan lined with floured wax paper. Using a 2 ½ to 3-inch round cutter or drinking glass, cut rounds. Transfer rounds to the floured baking sheet. Repeat with the dough scraps until most of the dough has been used. You can roll the very last dough scraps into firm balls and pat them flat so they look similar to the rest of the rounds.

Cover the dough with a tea towel and let it rise in a warm place for about 30-45 minutes or until they have puffed up noticeably. This is important – if you don't let them rise long enough, they will not be high and fluffy in the end. Uncover them for the last 15 minutes so they will dry a little (only a little!) and will develop a "skin".

Once the dough is risen, heat 1 to 2 inches of oil in a medium saucepan over medium heat until it reaches 320-330 °F degrees. A cooking or deep frying thermometer comes in handy here but I've already made Krapfen without. It takes a little adjusting though… Dip a wooden skewer/chopstick or handle of a wooden cooking spoon into the hot oil to test the temperature. If the oil starts steadily bubbling, then the oil is hot enough for frying. (bubbling vigorously = too hot, very few bubbles = not hot enough). As always: Be careful handling hot oil!

Using a flat spatula, carefully slip 3 rounds into the oil, upside down. Cover the saucepan so the Krapfen can rise further and will get a nice, white ring. Fry until golden, about 1 ½ to 2 minutes. Turn Krapfen over with a slotted spatula and fry uncovered until golden on the other side. Carefully transfer the Krapfen to a paper towel-lined baking sheet with a slotted spatula. Process the same way with the rest of the dough.

Let the Krapfen cool. Place the jam in a piping bag with a round tip. Stick a skewer or chopstick in the side of the Krapfen to create a tunnel. Pipe in some of the jam.

Dust the Doughnuts with confectioners' sugar. They taste best eaten on the same day.

Recipe from www.lilvienna.com/krapfen-austrian-jam-filled-donuts/

LAMB'S WOOL

Made on Twelfth Night.

> 6 baking apples, cored
> 2 Tablespoons to 1/2 cup brown
>   sugar
> 2 quarts sweet cider or hard cider
> 1/8 teaspoon nutmeg
> 1/4 teaspoon cinnamon
> 1/4 teaspoon ground ginger

Roast the apples in a baking pan at 450 degrees for about an hour, or until they are soft and begin to burst. You may leave the apples whole or break them up.

In a large saucepan, dissolve the sugar, a few tablespoons at a time, in the cider or ale, tasting for sweetness. Add the spices. Bring the liquid to a boil, lower the heat, and simmer for 10 to 15 minutes. Pour the liquid over the apples in a large punchbowl, or serve in large mugs.

Recipe from A Continual Feast

MEXICAN HOT CHOCOLATE

Made throughout the Christmas season and on Twelfth Night.

> For the hot chocolate
> 2 cups milk (I used 2%)
> 2 tablespoons unsweetened cocoa
>   powder
> 2 tablespoons granulated sugar
> 1/2 teaspoon ground cinnamon
> 1/4 teaspoon vanilla extract
> 1/8 teaspoon chili powder
> 1/8 teaspoon ground cayenne
>   (optional - you can omit this if you
>   don't want it too spicy)
> 1 ounce bittersweet chocolate

Optional toppings
marshmallows, chocolate shavings,
cinnamon stick for stirring

In a medium saucepan over medium-high heat, add milk, cocoa powder, sugar, cinnamon, vanilla extract, chili powder, and cayenne pepper (if desired).

Mix together with a whisk, add the bittersweet chocolate, and heat until the chocolate has completely melted and the mixture is hot, but not boiling.

Divide hot chocolate into 2 mugs and serve with marshmallows, chocolate shavings, and a cinnamon stick.

Recipe from www.isabeleats.com/mexican-hot-chocolate/

MULLED ALE

Served on St. Stephen's Day.

18 oz Christmas ale (or Altbier, bock
lager, winter warmer ale)
2 1/2 tbsp dark brown sugar 4-6
cloves to taste
2 star anise
1 cinnamon stick
1/2 tsp ground nutmeg
6 pieces orange peel, thin top layer of
skin only, without the bitter white
layer

3 oz brandy, substitute with Cognac if
you feel like splurging

In a saucepan or small pot mix the ale (one and a half
bottles, 18 oz total) with the brown sugar and nutmeg,
add the cloves, star anise, cinnamon stick, and orange
peel.

Bring to a gentle simmer (do not allow to boil), stir for
sugar to dissolve, and let simmer for 2-3 min to become
well-infused with the spices.

Remove from heat and add the brandy.

Serve in mugs, garnished with an orange slice.

Recipe from

www.craftbeering.com/mulled-ale-recipe-brandy/

MULLED CIDER

Made on Christmas Eve and Christmas Day.

2 quarts cider or apple juice
Peel of one orange or 2 teaspoons
orange extract
1 to 2 sticks of cinnamon
1/2 tsp. allspice
1/2 tsp. cloves

Put all ingredients in a saucepan and bring to a boil. Lower the heat and simmer 5 to 10 minutes.

PANETTONE (ITALIAN CHRISTMAS BREAD)

Made on Christmas Eve and Christmas Day.

Marinated fruit:

> 1/3 cup golden raisins
> 1/3 cup chopped dried apricots
> 1/3 cup dried tart cherries
> 1/4 cup triple sec (orange-flavored liqueur) or orange juice

Dough:

> 1 package dry yeast (about 2 1/4 teaspoons)
> 1/4 teaspoon granulated sugar
> 1/4 cup warm water (100° to 110°)
> 3 3/4 cups all-purpose flour, divided
> 6 tablespoons butter or stick margarine, melted
> 1/4 cup whole milk
> 1/4 cup granulated sugar
> 1/2 teaspoon salt
> 1 large egg
> 1 large egg yolk
> 2 tablespoons pine nuts

Cooking spray
1 teaspoon butter, melted
2 teaspoons sugar

To prepare marinated fruit, combine the first 4 ingredients in a small bowl; let stand for 1 hour. Drain fruit in a sieve over a bowl, reserving fruit and 2 teaspoons liqueur separately.

To prepare dough, dissolve yeast and 1/4 teaspoon granulated sugar in warm water in a small bowl; let stand 5 minutes. Lightly spoon flour into dry measuring cups; level with a knife. Combine 1/2 cup flour and next 6 ingredients (1/2 cup flour through egg yolk) in a large bowl; beat at medium speed of a mixer 1 minute or until smooth. Add yeast mixture and 1/2 cup flour; beat 1 minute. Stir in marinated fruit, 2 1/2 cups flour, and pine nuts.

Turn dough out onto a lightly floured surface. Knead until smooth and elastic (about 8 minutes); add enough of remaining flour, 1 tablespoon at a time, to prevent dough from sticking to hands. Place dough in a large bowl coated with cooking spray, turning to coat top. Cover and let rise in a warm place (85°), free from drafts, about 1 1/2 hours. Dough will not double in size. (Press two fingers into dough. If indentation remains, the dough has risen enough.) Punch dough down; let rest 5 minutes.

Divide in half, shaping each into a ball. Place balls into 2

(13-ounce) coffee cans coated with cooking spray. Cover and let rise 1 hour.

Preheat oven to 375°. Uncover dough. Place coffee cans on bottom rack in oven, and bake at 375° for 30 minutes or until browned and loaf sounds hollow when tapped. Remove bread from cans, and cool on a wire rack. Combine reserved 2 teaspoons liqueur and 1 teaspoon butter; brush over loaves. Sprinkle evenly with sugar.

Recipe from myrecipes.com

PASSATELLI IN BRODO

Made on the Feast of Saint Stephen.

> 4 cups stale breadcrumbs
> 2 cups Parmigiano cheese
> 4 Eggs
> ½ of a lemon zested
> 1 tsp nutmeg freshly grated
> Pinch of salt
> 8 1/2 cups chicken stock

Place the breadcrumbs, parmesan, and flour on a wooden board. Stir with your hands to combine and make a well in the center.

Crack the eggs into the center of the well. Add the lemon zest, nutmeg, and pinch of salt.

Using a fork slowly work the eggs around incorporating the breadcrumb mixture. Work the eggs into a dough and knead for 3 minutes. If the dough is a little wet add a little flour until the dough comes together.

Cover the dough and allow to rest for a minimum of 10 minutes.

Place your chicken stock into a pot and bring to a boil whilst you prepare the passatelli pasta.

Cut the dough into small workable sections.

Press each section of dough through a traditional passatelli press or use a potato ricer with holes that should be 5mm in diameter (larger than a standard potato ricer).

Pass the passatelii through the press and cut them with a sharp knife when they are 4cm in length. Lay them gently onto a tea towel and continue until you have used all of the prepared dough.

Cook the passatelli in the stock for around 3 minutes. Ladle into bowls, scatter with additional Parmesan, and fall in love.

Carmela's tip: When making Passatelli it is essential that the breadcrumbs are stale and the bread contains no olive oil as this will affect the overall cooking of the passatelli, making them fall apart. Many chefs also add a little 00 flour to their passatelli dough to help in combining the dough, feel free to do this but this is cheating!

Recipe from www.carmelas-kitchen.com

PERNIL

Made on Christmas Eve for the Noche Buena feast.

> 1 (7-pound) bone-in or boneless pork
>   shoulder
> ¼ cup vegetable or canola oil
> 12 cloves garlic minced
> ¼ cup <u>fresh oregano leaves</u>
> 1 tablespoon dried oregano
> 2 tablespoons Adobo seasoning the
>   powdered canned kind
> 1 tablespoon paprika
> teaspoon kosher salt plus more for
>   seasoning at the end
> ½ teaspoon freshly ground black
>   pepper plus more for seasoning at
>   the end
> Juice of 2 lemons and 1 orange

Score the fat on the pork shoulder in a criss-cross hatch fashion. Then, cut deeply once in each direction across the pork, like you are going to cut it into four quarters, but then leave them attached at the bottom. Use a sharp knife to make about 20 slits, about 1 inch deep, all over the meat. Place the meat in a 13 x 9 baking pan, or another shallow baking pan large enough to comfortably hold the meat with some space around it.

Combine the oil, garlic, fresh and dried oregano, Adobo, paprika, salt and pepper. Rub the mixture all over the meat, working it all over the surface and into the slits. Cover the pork with foil and refrigerate overnight.

Bring the pork to room temperature, about 1 hour. Meanwhile, preheat the oven to 300F°. Bake the pork, covered for 3 hours, then remove the foil and bake for another 3 to 4 hours at the same temperature, until the pork is fall-apart tender. The internal temperature should be at least 165°, but it may be higher, which is fine – it's most important that the meat is super tender. If you would like a crustier exterior, turn the heat to 375°F and bake for another 20 to 30 minutes, until the outside of the pork has a nice browned crust.

Let the pernil sit for at least 20 minutes, then use your fingers (if it's not too hot; some people like to wear kitchen gloves to protect their fingers from the heat), or two forks to pull the meat into chunks. Sprinkle the meat with lemon and orange juice, season with additional salt and pepper, and serve hot or warm.

Recipe from www.themom100.com

PONCHE (MEXICAN CHRISTMAS PUNCH)

Made on Christmas Eve and Christmas Day.

4 quarts water

2 cinnamon sticks

8 whole cloves

5 long tamarind pods, husk removed, and seeded or boil the entire pod to make removing easier

½ pound tejocotes or crab apples, left whole

6 large guavas, peeled and cut into large bite-size chunks

2 red apples (of your choice), peeled, cored, and cut into small bite-size chunks

1 pear (of your choice), peeled, cored, and cut into small bite-size chunks

2 (4-inch) sugarcane sticks, peeled and cut into small chunks

1 cup pitted prunes

1/2 cup dark raisins

1 orange, sliced

1 cone piloncillo, chopped or 1 cup dark brown sugar

1 ounce brandy or tequila per cup (optional)

In a large pot, over high heat, boil water, cinnamon sticks, cloves, tamarind, and tejocotes. After it starts to boil, lower the heat and simmer for about 10 minutes until the tejocotes are soft. Remove the tejocotes from the heat, peel, remove hard ends, cut in half, and deseed. Return them to the pot. Add guavas, apples, pears, sugar cane, prunes, orange slices, and piloncillo. Simmer for at least 30 minutes, stirring gently. Discard cinnamon sticks and cloves. Ladle into cups, making sure each cup gets some chunks of fruit. Add brandy or tequila to each cup (optional).

Recipe from muybuenocooking.com

RICE CAKES WITH LOUISIANA SYRUP (CANE SYRUP)

For breakfast on Christmas morning.

2 cups cooked rice
1 ½ teaspoons baking powder
½ teaspoon salt
1 tablespoon sugar
½ teaspoon cinnamon
½ teaspoon grated whole nutmeg
1 ¼ cups all-purpose flour
3 large eggs, lightly beaten
2 tablespoons vegetable oil

Place the rice in a medium bowl. Stir in baking powder, salt, sugar, cinnamon, nutmeg, and flour. Gradually to rice mixture, stirring with a whisk until well-blended.

Heat oil in a large skillet over medium heat. Drop rice mixture by level tablespoonfuls into the pan. Cook for 4 minutes on each side or until golden. Remove fritters from the pan with a slotted spoon. Pat dry with paper towels. Serve immediately with Louisiana Cane Syrup.

Recipe from

www.dkajunprincess.wordpress.com

ROAST GOOSE

Made on Christmas Day.

> 1 pound (approx 22) dried pears
> 1¾ cups fresh cranberries (or, if
>   frozen, thawed)
> 1 cup dried breadcrumbs
> ½ teaspoon ground cinnamon
> ¼ teaspoon ground cloves
> 1 teaspoon ground ginger
> zest and pulpy juice of 1 clementine
>   or satsuma
> 1 onion (peeled and chopped)
> 2 tablespoons maple syrup
> 1 cup pecan nuts
> 1 tablespoon kosher salt

1 x 11 lb fresh goose

Either soak the dried pears overnight in cold water or pour boiling water over them and leave to cool; this will take 2-3 hours.

Drain the pears and put them into a bowl along with the cranberries and breadcrumbs.

Add the cinnamon, cloves, ginger and clementine/satsuma zest and pulp.

Stir in the chopped onion, maple syrup, and pecans, and add the salt.

Make sure everything is thoroughly mixed before you stuff the goose.

Preheat your oven to 425°F.

Remove any excess fat from the goose cavity — this can go towards your roast potatoes — and remove the neck and giblets, reserving them for the gravy.

Stuff the cavity of the goose with the pear and cranberry stuffing and, once stuffed, wrap the goose skin over, securing it with a skewer.

Sit the stuffed goose on a wire rack in a fairly deep roasting tin, as the goose will give off a lot of fat as it cooks and you don't want spillage. Once the fat has cooled, keep in the fridge: it is wonderful for any frying and roasting.

Cook the goose for 3 hours (after about an hour, drain off the excess fat in the tin, and again every half hour or so).

Remove to a board and carve judiciously.

Recipe from www.nigella.com

ST. JOHN'S WINE

Made on the Feast of St. John.

> 1 quart red wine
> 3 whole cloves
> 1/16 teaspoon ground cardamom
> 2 two-inch cinnamon sticks
> 1/2 teaspoon ground nutmeg
> 1/2 cup sugar

Pour the wine into a large saucepan. Add the remaining ingredients. Boil for 5 minutes (at this point the alcohol will be pretty much evaporated). Serve hot.

ST. STEPHEN'S HORSESHOES

Made on the Feast of St. Stephen.

Dough Ingredients

> 1 tablespoon dry yeast
> 1/2 cup milk, lukewarm (100-110 degrees)

3 eggs

1 cup sour cream

2 teaspoons lemon juice

Grated rind of 2 lemons

1 cup cold butter, chopped into small
    pieces

5 cups flour

2/3 cups sugar

1/2 teaspoon salt

1/2 cup shortening

Filling Ingredients

1 1 /2 - 2 cups walnuts, finely
    chopped

½ - 3/4 cup brown sugar

1 egg

1/2 teaspoon vanilla

grated rind of 1 orange

grated rind of 1 lemon

Dissolve yeast in the lukewarm milk and let stand for 10 minutes.

In a large mixing bowl, beat the eggs until light and fluffy. Stir in the sour cream, yeast mixture, lemon juice and rind.

In another mixing bowl, combine the flour, sugar, and salt. Cut the cold butter into small pieces. Using either a pastry blender, two knives, or your hands, work the butter and shortening into the flour mixture until it resembles coarse bread crumbs.

Add the flour mixture to the moist ingredients and beat well. You may need to add more flour, just enough to make a fairly soft and non-sticky dough, depending on the size of the eggs.

Knead dough briefly. Wrap in plastic wrap and chill for 1 hour.

While the dough is chilling, prepare the filling. Chop the nuts finely. (We used walnuts, but hazelnuts or almonds would work great too!) Combine the brown sugar, egg, vanilla and rinds, then stir in the nuts.

On a lightly floured surface, roll the dough out to about 1/8 inch thickness and cut into 4x6 inch rectangles.

Brush the rectangles with some melted butte (I actually skipped this step) and spread a thin layer of filling in the middle. Starting on the long side, roll each rectangle and form into the shape of a horseshoe. (Note: As you can see in my pictures above, the filling did ooze out of some of the horseshoes in my first batch. On the following batches, I made sure the dough was pinched together to prevent this from happening again.)

Place on a lightly greased baking sheet. Bake at 375°F for about 15 minutes or until the horseshoes are nicely browned.

Dust with powdered sugar or glaze with a mixture of lemon juice and powdered sugar if desired.

Recipe from A Continual Feast.

STOLLEN

Made on Christmas Eve and throughout the season of Christmastide.

Stollen has been made in Germany since the Middle Ages. When you fold the dough, instead of turning the folds underneath, you leave them on top to resemble Jesus's swaddling clothes!

> 2/3 cup dark raisins
> 2/3 cup golden raisins
> 1/2 cup dried cranberries or cherries
> 1/3 cup dark rum or orange juice
> 1 cup slivered or sliced almonds,
>   lightly toasted
> 1/4 cup water
> 2 1/2 teaspoons powdered yeast
> 1/2 cup milk (whole or low-fat) at
>   room temperature
> 3 1/2 cups all-purpose flour
> 1/2 cup rye flour, or use similar
>   amount all-purpose flour
> 1/2 cup plus 3 tablespoons sugar
> 1 1/2 teaspoons ground dried ginger
> 1 teaspoon sea salt

1 teaspoon ground cinnamon

1 teaspoon ground cardamom

1 teaspoon freshly-grated nutmeg

1 teaspoon grated lemon or orange zest, preferably unsprayed

3/4 teaspoon vanilla bean paste or extract

1 cup plus 3/4 cup unsalted butter, melted

1 tablespoon honey

1 large egg yolk

1/2 cup chopped candied ginger

1/2 cup diced candied citrus peel

1/2 cup powdered sugar or more, if necessary

Mix both kinds of raisins with cranberries or cherries with the dark rum or orange juice, then cover. In another bowl, mix the almonds with the water, and cover. Let both sit for at least an hour, or overnight.

Pour the milk into a medium bowl and sprinkle the yeast over it. Stir briefly, then stir in 1 cup of the flour until smooth to make a starter. Cover, and let rest for one hour.

In the bowl of a stand mixer, with the paddle attachment, or by hand, stir together the remaining 2 1/2 cups flour, rye flour, 3 tablespoons sugar, 1/2 teaspoon of dried ginger, salt, cinnamon, cardamom, nutmeg, citrus zest, and vanilla. Pour in 1 cup of the melted butter, honey, and egg yolk, and mix on medium speed until the mixture is moistened uniformly.

While mixing, add the yeast starter, one-third at a time, mixing until thoroughly incorporated. Once added, continue to beat for about four minutes until almost smooth: it should resemble cookie dough. Add the dried fruits (and any liquid), candied ginger, citrus peel, and almonds, and beat until they're well-distributed

Turn the dough out onto a lightly floured surface and knead a few times, then place back in the mixer bowl, cover, and let rest in a warm place for one hour.

Remove the dough from the bowl, knead the dough again, then return it to the bowl. Let rest for another hour.

Divide the dough into four pieces shape each one into an oval, and place them evenly spaced apart on an insulated baking sheet.

(The original recipe says to stack two rimmed baking sheets on top of each other, so you can do that if you don't have one.)

Cover the loaves with a clean tea towel and let rest in a warm place for one hour.

Preheat the oven to 350F. Remove the tea towel and bake the loaves for 45 minutes, or until they're deep golden brown. (Note: The recipe advises that when they're done, the internal temperature should read 190F if using an instant-read thermometer.)

While the loaves are baking, mix together the remaining 1/2 cup sugar and 1 teaspoon dried ginger. When the bread comes out of the oven, generously brush the remaining 3/4 cup melted butter over the hot loaves, letting the butter saturate the bread, repeating until all the butter is absorbed.

Rub the gingered sugar mixture over the top and side of each loaf then let rest on the baking sheet until room temperature.

Sift powdered sugar over, under, and around the bread, rubbing it in with your hands. They wrap the loaves on the baking sheet in a large plastic bag and let them sit for two days. After two days, the loaves are ready to eat or can be wrapped as gifts. You may wish to sift additional powdered sugar over the top in case they need another dusting.

Recipe from www.davidlebovitz.com/stollen/

SYLVESTER PUNCH

Made on New Year's Eve.

> 2 oranges, grated rind, and juice
> 2 lemons, grated rind and juice
> Sugar to taste (about 1 cup)
> 4 cups white wine
> 2 cups light rum

Grate the orange and lemon rinds. Combine with the sugar, wine and rum in a large saucepan. Add with the strained juices of the orange and lemon. Heat (do not boil). Serve hot.

Recipe from A Continual Feast

TAMALES

Made on Christmas Eve and Christmas Day.

Tamale Filling:

> 1 1/4 pounds pork loin
> 1 large onion, halved
> 1 clove garlic
> 4 dried California chile pods
> 2 cups water
> 1 1/2 teaspoons salt

Tamale Dough:

> 2 cups masa harina
> 1 (10.5 ounce) can beef broth
> 1 teaspoon baking powder
> 1/2 teaspoon salt
> 2/3 cup lard
> 1 (8 ounce) package dried corn husks
> 1 cup sour cream

Place pork into a Dutch oven with onion and garlic, and add water to cover. Bring to a boil, then reduce heat to low and simmer until the meat is cooked through, about 2 hours.

Use rubber gloves to remove stems and seeds from the chile pods. Place chiles in a saucepan with 2 cups of water. Simmer, uncovered, for 20 minutes, then remove from heat to cool. Transfer the chiles and water to a blender and blend until smooth. Strain the mixture, stir in salt, and set aside. Shred the cooked meat and mix in one cup of the chile sauce.

Soak the corn husks in a bowl of warm water. In a large bowl, beat the lard with a tablespoon of the broth until fluffy. Combine the masa harina, baking powder and salt; stir into the lard mixture, adding more broth as necessary to form a spongy dough.

Spread the dough out over the corn husks to 1/4 to 1/2 inch thickness. Place one tablespoon of the meat filling into the center. Fold the sides of the husks in toward the center and place in a steamer. Steam for 1 hour.

Remove tamales from husks and drizzle remaining chile sauce over. Top with sour cream. For a creamy sauce, mix sour cream into the chile sauce.

Recipe from allrecipes.com

THREE KINGS CAKE OR ROSCA DE REYES

Made on Twelfth Night or Epiphany.

> 1/2 cup of warm water
> 1 envelope or 2 ¼ teaspoons of active
>   yeast
> 4 cups all-purpose flour plus 2 or 3
>   tablespoons more for dusting
> ¾ cup of sugar
> 3 large eggs
> 3 egg yolks mixed with 4 tablespoons
>   of milk
> ¼ teaspoon salt
> 2 tablespoons orange water or 1 1/2
>   tablespoons orange extract
> 1 ½ stick unsalted butter softened
> Freshly grated orange zest from one
>   orange
> 1 plastic baby doll or a dried bean

Sugared Oranges:

> Thinly sliced oranges
> 1/2 cup sugar
> Enough water to cover the orange
>   slices

Glaze:

> 1 egg beaten for glazing the bread
> 1 tablespoon whole milk or water
> White sugar to sprinkle on top of the
>   bread
> 2 or 3 plastic baby dolls

To make the sugared oranges, thinly slice oranges and then cut them in half. Place in a saucepan with water and sugar and bring to a boil. Reduce to a low boil and cook for 30 minutes. Drain the orange slices on a cookie rack and allow to cool.

To make the bread, put your lukewarm water into a bowl, and sprinkle with yeast. Stir with a fork until yeast has dissolved, then let stand until foamy, 5 to 10 minutes. Stir in ½ cup of the flour, and cover the bowl with plastic wrap. Let stand in a warm place until doubled in bulk, about 25 minutes.

In the meantime, mix flour, eggs, egg yolks, sugar, orange extract, orange zest, salt, and butter in a large bowl. Mix until crumbly. Add yeast mixture to the bowl and mix. It will be very sticky but manageable, add flour if needed. Place on a lightly floured surface and start kneading until you have a smooth dough. It will take about 15-20 minutes to get these results or 7 minutes in a stand mixer. DO NOT add too much flour to your working area, the texture should be very soft, sort of wet but manageable. If you add more flour than needed your bread will be dry.

Once your dough is smooth and soft, place in a buttered bowl, and cover with buttered plastic wrap. The dough must be wet and elastic. Let dough stand in a warm place until doubled in volume, about 1 and ½ hours. If the dough doesn't double in volume after this time let it rest longer.

After the first resting period. Turn the dough out onto a lightly floured surface, and knead a few times, then shape it into a round cushion and make a hole in the middle to shape it into a large ring. Transfer to a greased-rimmed baking sheet, and loosely cover with buttered plastic wrap. Let rise in a warm place for 45 minutes or more until almost double in volume. Gather all your decorations and the egg wash. For the egg wash whisk the remaining egg with milk or water.

Preheat oven for at least 20 minutes before baking at 375 degrees, with rack in the lower third.

Brush the dough with the egg wash two times for a golden crust. Place the sugared orange slices around the ring, pressing them gently into the dough. Sprinkle with sugar and bake for 10 minutes. Reduce heat to 350 degrees and bake for 10 more minutes until bread is a nice golden brown color. Depending on your oven it will require more time.

Transfer the bread to a wire rack to cool. After the bread has cooled insert the plastic baby doll or bean from the bottom of the bread. Do not forget to let your guests know that there is a baby toy or bean inside the bread.

The bread can be stored in an airtight container for up to 3 days.

WASSAIL

Served on Twelfth Night.

2 apples
8 cups apple cider
2 cups orange juice
1/3 cup lemon juice
4 cinnamon sticks
15 whole cloves, or 1/2 tsp ground
cloves
1/4 teaspoon ground ginger
1/4 teaspoon ground nutmeg
1 Tablespoon light brown sugar,
optional

Poke the whole cloves into the apples on all sides. Add all of the ingredients, including the apples, to a large pot over medium-low heat. Bring to a simmer. Simmer for 30-45 minutes. Remove the apples and whole cloves. Ladle into mugs and enjoy!

Recipe from www.tastesbetterfromscratch.com/hot-wassail/

Made in the USA
Middletown, DE
09 November 2024

64215206R00102